## DATE DUE

| | |
|---|---|
| | |
| | |
| | |
| | |
| | |
| | |
| | |
| | |
| | |
| | |
| | |
| | |
| | |
| | |
| | |
| | |
| | |

BRODART, CO.                    Cat. No. 23-221

# LIVING IN...
# ANCIENT ROME

# LIVING IN...
# ANCIENT ROME

Series consultant editor: Norman Bancroft Hunt

CHELSEA HOUSE
PUBLISHERS
An imprint of Infobase Publishing

**LIVING IN ANCIENT ROME**

Text and design © 2009 Thalamus Publishing

Chelsea House
An imprint of Infobase Publishing
132 West 31st Street
New York, NY 10001

**Library of Congress Cataloging-in-Publication Data**

Bancroft-Hunt, Norman.
  Living in ancient Rome / Norman Bancroft-Hunt. — 1st ed.
    p. cm. — (Living in the ancient world)
  Includes index.
  ISBN 978-0-8160-6340-6
  1. Rome—Civilization—Juvenile literature. I. Title.
  DG77.B33 2008
  937--dc22

                            2008009490

Chelsea House books are available at special discounts when purchased in bulk quantities for businesses, associations, institutions or sales promotions. Please call our Special Sales Department in New York at (212) 967-8800 or (800) 322-8755.

You can find Chelsea House on the World Wide Web at http://www.chelseahouse.com

For Thalamus Publishing
Series consultant editor: Norman Bancroft Hunt
Contributors: Nick Constable, Roger Kean, Angus Konstam, Warren Lapworth
Project editor: Warren Lapworth
Maps and design: Roger Kean

Printed and bound in China

10  9  8  7  6  5  4  3  2  1
This book is printed on acid-free paper

**Picture acknowledgments**
All illustrations by Oliver Frey except for – Jean-Claude Golvin: 58 (below), 67 (above); John James/Temple Rogers: 88-89 (left); Roger Kean/Thalamus: 14–15 (all), 52 (all), 53 (below), 65, 74 (above), 75 (with Oliver Frey), 91 (above), 92 (inset); Mike White/Temple Rogers: 29 (panel, both), 38, 43 (top), 48, 51, 53 (top), 54–55, 56–57 (below), 62–63, 67 (below), 72, 82.

Photographs – Corbis: 8–9; Araldo de Luca/Corbis: 38, 46–47, 50, 51, 75, 93 (all); Mimmo Jodice/Corbis: 33 (below right), 39 (center); Roger Kean/Thalamus: 2, 12 (both), 29 (above), 34-35 (center), 48, 49, 61, 65, 74 (below), 77.

# CONTENTS

# Place in History

6000 BCE
4000 BCE
3500 BCE
2340 BCE
1900 BCE
1600 BCE
1100 BCE
539 BCE

**MESOPOTAMIA**

3100 BCE
2686 BCE
2200 BCE
2040 BCE
1782 BCE
1570 BCE
1070 BCE
747 BCE
332 BCE
30 BCE

**EGYPT**

2600 BCE
1100 BCE
800 BCE
500 BCE
146 BCE

**GREECE**

753 BCE
509 BCE
27 BCE

**ROME**

# What Rome Did for Us

In a history of over 1200 years, Rome grew from a primitive settlement on the Tiber's banks into the most powerful empire of the ancient world. Rome provided Europe, much of the Middle East, and North Africa with a unified social, legal, and administrative system, as well as a common language that was the basis of many European tongues thereafter. The Romans quantified time and the calendar, they gave Europe a superb road network, concrete bridges, a postal system, central heating, piped fresh water, enormous public baths, and monumental civic buildings. In the Roman world, we see the culmination of ancient Eurasian culture in about every respect that can be imagined.

# Italy's Landscape and Climate

At its peak, the Roman Empire spanned from Scotland to Iraq, from Romania to Morocco. But it is the geography of Italy that dictated Roman culture and civilization.

In some respects, Italy shares many geographical similarities with Greece. As a peninsula, it has a great deal of coastline relative to its total area. Unlike the Greeks, however, the Roman never became happy seafarers. Italy is also a mountainous place—only about one-fifth of the land is classified as plain, much of which is concentrated in the valley of the River Po.

To the north, Italy is cut off from the rest of Europe by the barrier of the Alps, while the Apennines running down the center split the peninsula into two unequal halves. Running closer to the eastern seaboard, the Apennines reduce the coastal plain to a narrow strip, poor for agriculture.

Add to this the few and small rivers that run into the Adriatic Sea, which often dry up in the hot summers, and it is easy to see why ancient settlements were few and far between to the east of the mountains.

By contrast, the wider plains of the Tyrrhenian coast west of the Apennines region, especially in the Campania, were capable of supporting a greater concentration of agriculture. Two respectably sized rivers—the Tiber and Arno—provided a plentiful water supply and a means of navigation inland.

The farming land supported a wide range of livestock and market gardening, but there was less land for growing cereals. As the population increased, Italy came to rely on alternative sources for grain to mill for bread flour, first Sicily, then North Africa and—most importantly—Egypt. This reliance on overseas sources posed a threat to Rome when, for one reason or another, the supply was interrupted. A failure of the grain supply inevitably led to riots in the streets.

In ancient times, while the Po valley was a fertile region, most of the eastern half was subject to heavy flooding in the winters and marshy for much of the year. As a result, civilizations grew up on the western side, as they did in the center.

To the south, the Calabrian region is mountainous, and the eastern Apulian area is arid through lack of rainfall, so neither was suited to nurturing civilization.

The main lines of communication in central Italy from the coast to the interior were along the rivers, especially the Tiber. The most strategic point on the river, the highest point for heavy river traffic to reach and the lowest crossing point to connect with the north-south coastal traffic, was where legendary Romulus plowed a sacred furrow and founded his tiny settlement.

Here, too, were plenty of resources, good pine and beech trees for timber, stone for building, and clay pits for making tiles, bricks, and pottery.

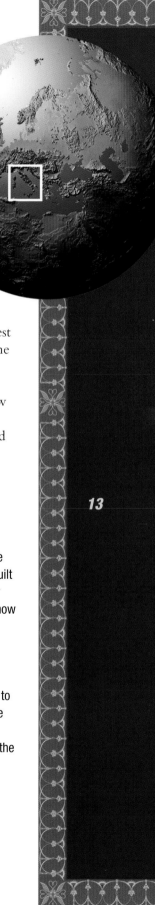

**13**

1. Cerveteri (Caeare)
2. Veii
3. Fidenae
4. Ostia (Antiqua)
5. Rome
6. Tibur (Tivoli)
7. Lavinum
8. Ardea
9. Alba Longa
10. Lanuvium
11. Velitrae (birthplace of Augustus)
12. Antium (birthplace of Caligula)

*13. Tyrrhenian Sea*
*14.* Site of Portus, the new port for Rome built by Claudius and later extended by Trajan (now Rome's international airport).
*15. Lake Bracciano*
*16. River Tiber* (artificially enhanced to make its course more visible).
*17.* Western edge of the Appenine Mountains
*18. Lake Alba*

# A Brief History of Rome, 753 BCE–CE 476

Rome's history is one of increasingly sophisticated administrative and political institutions controlling a "citizen-army" that dominated the known world of the West.

Long before the Romans, a great part of the western seaboard was occupied by the Etruscans. This mysterious people had already developed a sophisticated civilization, with substantial cities, paved roads, sewage systems, and complex religious and funerary rites. The Romans later borrowed heavily from the Etruscans.

Other tribes coexisted with the Etruscans—Samnites, Umbrians, Sabines, and Latins. In its earliest phase, the area around the small settlement of Rome was shared between these tribes, and Rome's kings were drawn from among the Latins, Sabines, and Etruscans. Tradition states that Romulus

created the institution of a Senate to be the king's advisors.

## Birth of a Republic

At about the same time that Athens experimented with democracy, the senators tired of the tyrannical reign of Etruscan king Lucius Tarquinius II and threw him out. In his place they created a government called *respublica*, meaning "a matter for the people".

As Rome's "luck" drew in more of the neighboring villages, so the pressure on land increased and Rome began competing with more distant settlements. Following the Greek example, Roman expansion took the

**Rome c.500 BCE**

**1.** Sublican bridge over the Tiber.

**2.** Portus (harbor).

**3.** Forum Boarium (beef market).

**4.** Circus Maximus.

**5.** Tarpeian Rock (traitors are thrown from it).

**Rome c.500 BCE**

Eventual route of the Appian Way

rm of founding colonies at the edges of thers' territory, and then taking it over. etween 499 and 290 numerous wars rought Rome the control of Latium, the Apennines, and most of Campania.

Between 280 and 272, the Greek colonies o the south were brought to heel, despite he aid of King Pyrrhus of Epirus, who rought over an army to help the Greeks. He won battles but lost more men than the Romans and finally Pyrrhus returned home.

## War with Carthage

n the next stage of expansion, Roman mbitions turned toward the Greek-Carthaginian island of Sicily, which sparked ff the three Punic Wars. Romans called the Carthaginians of North Africa *Poeni*, meaning Phoenicians, and the First Punic War raged in 264–241. Carthage was a naval ower, and for the first time the Roman

**6.** Capitol hill with Temple of Jupiter.

**7.** Arx with Temple of Juno Moneta.

**8.** Palatine, later filled by the imperial palaces.

**9.** Forum Romanum, subject to flooding from the gulch between the Capitol and Palatine.

**10.** Subura district

**11.** Cemetery

**12.** Field of Mars

**13.** Servian Wall

**Geographic features:**
**A** Caelian Hill
**B** Aventine Hill
**C** Lake Camenarum
**D** Quirinal Hill
**E** Viminal Hill
**F** Esquiline Hill
**G** Oppian Hill

military machine had to cope with the sea and ships. Innovation won out over sailors' fear and inexperience, and Carthage was forced to sue for peace.

However, before long Carthage had built an empire in Spain, and it was from here that the nobleman Hannibal took the war back to Italy in 218, famously marching his army over the Alps during winter and taking the Romans by surprise. Hannibal raided almost freely throughout Italy for the next 15 years, defeating one Roman army after another and almost capturing Rome.

## Rome's growing empire

Rome fought back by invading Spain and eventually threatening Carthage itself. Hannibal was recalled from Italy and his army finally fell before the military skill of the Roman general Gnaeus Scipio. He landed in Africa in 203 and defeated Hannibal's army at Zama the following year.

For their part in supporting Carthage, the Macedonians were the next to feel Roman might. Springing from a beachhead on the Illyrian coast obtained between 229–219, Macedon was humbled in a series of wars, and by 146 all of Greece was a part of the expanding Roman Empire. In the same year Carthage was wiped out in the Third Punic

**The unification of Italy**

Roman territorial gains by:
- 500 BCE
- 290 BCE
- 272 BCE
- 218 BCE
- Greek-colonized area

Aquileia

Genoa

Ariminum

ADRIATIC SEA

CORSICA

Tarquinia

Rome

Capua

Naples

SARDINIA

TYRRHENIAN SEA

SICILY · Syracuse

Carthage ·

AFRICA

War. The site remained desolate until Julius Caesar founded a Roman colony there.

By the start of the 1st century BCE, the power of the legions and whoever commanded them had become the dominant factor in Roman politics. New men, often opposed to the Senate, fought each other for control. First Gaius Marius became dictator in 87 BCE, then Lucius Cornelius Sulla in 82. After him, Pompey "the Great," Crassus, and the young Julius Caesar vied for power. Caesar's military skills, honed during his astonishingly successful conquest of Gaul in 58–52, eventually brought him to the dictatorship in 47.

## The imperial era

But Caesar's ambitions made him many enemies in the Senate and when a group of Senators assassinated him in 44, it began a series of bitter civil wars. These lasted until 31 BCE, when Caesar's adopted son Octavian defeated his rival Mark Antony in a naval battle at Actium. It left Octavian undisputed ruler of the Roman Empire.

Because of his dominant position and a clever use of his power, in 27 BCE, Octavian was effectively handed the right of perpetual rule by the Senate, and given the title Augustus. The Julio-Claudian dynasty that Augustus founded ended with the suicide of the mad emperor Nero in 68 CE.

From this point on, Rome's history is one of succeeding dynasties conquering ever more territory, but also realizing a limit to expansion. The empire's very success attracted more and more "barbarian" tribes to gather enviously on its borders.

Later emperors proved unequal to the task of keeping the barbarians at bay, and the destruction by Goths of two-thirds of the Roman legions at Hadrianople in 378 CE paved the way for the eventual collapse of the Western Roman Empire in 476. The eastern half went on to become the Greek Byzantine Empire, which lasted until almost the end of the medieval period.

Dressed in their togas, Senators parade in a frieze on the *Ara Pacis Augustae* (Altar of Roman Peace), which celebrates the peace that Augustus Caesar, the first emperor, has brought to the world.

## The Roman classes

The people who live within the empire fall into two broad groups: *cives* (citizens) and *peregrini* (foreigners). In an earlier age "citizen" meant a free man who lived in the city of Rome or whose parents were both Romans, but by the time of Augustus (27 BCE–14 CE) many provincials were citizens.

Only citizens were allowed to vote in elections. Provincials did not have the full rights of citizens, but were expected to pay the taxes that citizens did not. This changed in the 3rd century CE, when citizenship was given to every free man in the empire.

Front of the Senate House or *Curia Julia*, built by Julius Caesar (K in the picture opposite). Standing in the Forum, it can hold all the Senators.

## Rome's social and political structure

The social and political systems that grew up during the period of the Republic (from 509 to 27 BCE) continued into the early imperial era. However, since this book is about the "ideal" Roman period CE 100–235, many of the famous institutions known from the late Republic had fallen into disuse by this time. It is, therefore, useful to look at how things happened in earlier time periods.

In the early imperial era, three classes of citizens are recognized. Patricians are descended from the "original" families of Rome, in effect the wealthy landowners and political leaders. Members of the Equestrian Order (knights) are called *equites*. They are descendants of the first Roman cavalry and

represent the middle class of businessmen and civil servants. *Plebeians*, or *plebs*, are the mass of poor citizens, descended from farmers and traders.

## Republican government

The original Senate was a body of a hundred men of patrician families. Later, the number of Senators increased until it reached 600. To be admitted to the Senate a man has to qualify by having a minimum income. Senators are forbidden to engage in trade, so their wealth comes from the ownership of land and the profits from agriculture.

Each year, the citizens in an election known as an Assembly, select certain senators to be government magistrates (officials).

## Plebeian power

In the 4th century BCE, the plebs challenged the patricians to be allowed to become senators and set up the *concilium plebis tributa*, or Popular Assembly. Each year the Assembly chose officials called "tribunes" to protect

their interests. Tribunes had the right to veto (stop) any law passed by the Senate that did not suit the plebs. In time, even plebs gained the right to become Senators and get elected as a consul—if they met the income qualification.

## Imperial government

As the first emperors gathered the various functions of government to themselves, many of the old institutions and magistracies fell into disuse. The tribunes were abolished (the emperor called himself the "people's tribune"). Consuls were chosen by the emperor, who also appointed his own provincial governors. The offices of *praetor*, *aedile*, and *quaestor* were incorporated within the imperial bureaucracy, and the Senate became little more than a debating club to advise (or hinder) the emperor.

Although toward the end of the Roman Empire the Senate had no real power to govern, it continued to exist until even after the fall of the Western Roman Empire.

13

# Table of Major Dates

## PEOPLE AND CULTURE

| 800 | 600 | 400 | 300 | 200 |
|---|---|---|---|---|
| • Rome founded by Romulus, centered on the Palatine Hill, April 21, 753<br>• Primitive huts on the Palatine<br>• Roman Forum laid out in the swamp between Palatine, Capitoline, and Quirinal Hills<br>• First stone buildings in Rome<br>• Ancus Marcius builds the first bridge across Tiber, c.620 | • Temple of Saturn (housing the treasury) is built in the Forum, 497<br>• Temple of Castor, 484<br>• Laws of the Twelve Tables, a codification of Roman law, are drawn up, 450 | • Walls around Rome's seven hills rebuilt and made stronger, 387<br>• First military road, the Appian Way, is begun, 312<br>• First aqueduct, the Aqua Appia, is built by Appius Claudius, c.310 | • Extensive building of temples in Rome | • Porcius Cato the Elder constructs th Basilica Porcia in t Roman Forum, c.1<br>• Basilica Aemilia and Aemilian Brid 179 |

*Statuette of a lictor official of the 3rd century BCE.*

## MAJOR TIME FRAMES

| Archaic Period, Age of Kings<br>753–509 | Early Republic<br>509–c.280 | Middle Republic<br>c.280–146 |
|---|---|---|

## MILITARY AND POLITICS

*The Lapis Niger stone, Rome's oldest public document, dates from c.500 BCE.*

*A section of the Aqua Appia, built in 310 BCE, which brought fresh water to Rome.*

| 800 | 600 | 400 | 300 | 200 |
|---|---|---|---|---|
| • The Sabine Numa Pompilius succeeds Romulus, 715–673<br>• Ancus Marcius expands Rome's population with peoples of conquered cities, 640–616<br>• Reign of Tarquin I, 616–579 | • Servius Tullius reorganizes army, tribes, and creates the *Comitia Centuriata*, 579–534<br>• Start of Roman Republic with ousting of Tarquin II, 509<br>• Romans defeat neighboring Latins at Lake Regillus, 499<br>• Magistrates and tribunes appointed to care for the city of Rome, 494<br>• Rome joins Latin League, 493 | • Ten-year siege of Veii ends as Romans take the Etruscan city, 396<br>• Gauls defeat Romans at Allia and then sack Rome, 387<br>• Patricians and plebeians share the consulship, 367<br>• Rome dissolves Latin League after defeating its members in the Latin War, 340–338<br>• Roman conquest and colonization of Italy begins, 334<br>• Second Samnite War, 327–304 | • Rome defeats Samnites (Third Samnite War), and gains mastery of central Italy, 298–290<br>• Committees of Plebs allowed to make laws without Senate approval, 287<br>• Pyrrhus of Epirus invades Italy, 280–275<br>• First Punic War with Carthage, Rome gains Sicily, 264–241<br>• Gauls invade Italy, defeated at Telamon, 255<br>• Second Punic War, 218–202<br>• Rome sides with Achaean League in Greece during the First Macedonian War, 214–205 | • Romans defeat Philip of Macedon, ending Second Macedonian War, 1<br>• Rome defeats Greek Seleucids at Thermopylae, drivi them from Europe, 191<br>• Third Punic War ends with destructi of Carthage,149–1<br>• Rome defeats Achaean League, destroys Corinth, a adds Greece to the empire, 146<br>• Southern Gaul is added to empire, 1<br>• Gaius Marius defeats Numidians North Africa, 106<br>• Against tradition, Marius is a consul seven times, 107, 104–100, and 86 |

| CE | 100 | 200 | 300 | 400 | 500 |
|---|---|---|---|---|---|

Theater of Pompey, 5; Forum of Julius Caesar, 46; Arch of Augustus, 21; Baths Agrippa (first major ublic baths), 19; heater of Marcellus, 7; Ara Pacis ugustae (peace tar), 9; Forum of ugustus, 2
Writers: Sallust, vy, Virgil, Horace, vid

eft: Head of Sulla.

- Flowering of latin literature: Lucan, Senecca, Martial, Pliny the Elder, Pliny the Younger, Tacitus, Josephus
- Christians are blamed for the Fire of Rome, 64
- Eruption of Vesuvius buries Pompeii and Herculaneum, 79
- Colosseum dedicated, 79

- Trajan's Forum and Market, 112
- Pantheon rebuilt, 118–128
- Hadrian's Villa at Tibur (Tivoli) 126–134
- Juvenal (satirist), Seutonius (historian), Apuleius (novelist)
- Hadrian codifies Roman Law, c.129

- Severus enhances his birthplace in North Africa, Leptis Magna
- Baths of Caracalla built at Rome, 216
- Aurelian builds new wall around Rome, 271
- Cassius Dio, Herodian (historians); Eusebius (Christian theologist)

*Coin of Constantine.*

- Persecution of Christians, 303–305
- Edict of Milan tolerates Christianity in the empire, 313
- Constantinople consecrated as new imperial capital, 330
- Julian "Apostate" fails to revive paganism, 361–363
- Claudian (poet); Lactantius (theologist and commentator); Ammianus Marcellinus (historian)

- Ravenna becomes Western imperial court, 402
- Last Roman forces leave Britain, which soon falls prey to Anglo-Saxon colonizers, 408
- Theodosian law code compiled, 429, and extended, 437

**ate Republic**
**146–30**

**Imperial Period**

**Western Empire**

**Eastern Empire**

Gaius Marius is ictator of Rome, 87 Social War, 91–89 Civil War between arius and Sulla, 3–86 Sulla is dictator of me, 82–80 Revolt of slaves led y Spartacus is put wn by Marcus rassus, 73–71 Caesar, Pompey, d Crassus form rst Triumvirate, 60 Caesar's army nquers Gaul, 58–52 Caesar is dictator Rome, 49–44 Second Triumvirate formed, 43 Octavian defeats ark Antony at tium, 31 Octavian takes ntrol of Rome, 27, comes Augustus

- Julio-Claudian emperors, 27 BCE–68 CE
- Conquest of Britain under Claudius, 43
- First Jewish revolt, 66–73
- Rebellion of Vindex in Gaul, 68
- Flavian emperors, 69–96
- Temple of Solomon in Jerusalem destroyed, 70
- Dacian Wars, 86–92

- Nervo-Trajanic emperors, 96–138
- Trajan invades Dacia, 101, adds it to the empire, 106
- Nabataea becomes the Roman province of Arabia, 106
- Second Jewish revolt, 132–135
- Antonine emperors, 138–192
- Germanic barbarians invade Danube frontier, 167
- Civil war brings Septimius Severus to the throne, 193–197

*Colosseum, 79.*

- Severan emperors, 193–235
- Reorganization of the army further removes senatorial control 200–211
- Caracalla extends citizenship to all free inhabitants of the provinces, 212
- Breakaway Gallic Empire, 259–273
- Queen Zenobia's Palmyrene rebellion, 266–272
- Aurelian abandons province of Dacia to the barbarians, 272
- Rebellion in Britain, 287–296
- Establishment of the Tetrarchy (rule of four) by Diocletian, 293

*Coin of Odoacer, King of Italy, 476.*

- Tetrarchic civil wars end with Constantine as sole ruler, 311–324
- Valentian dynasty, 364–392, later under dominion of Theodosian dynasty after 379
- Goths allowed to settle inside Danube frontier, 376
- Goths defeat Roman army of Valens at Hadrianople, 378
- Goths invade Greece, destroy Sparta, 395
- Division of the empire into East and West, 395

- Massed tribes of Germans cross Rhine and overrun Gaul, 406–407
- Vandals enter Spain, 409–428
- Alaric's Visigoths sack Rome, 410
- Toulouse becomes capital of Gothic kingdom in Gaul, 418
- Vandals cross to North Africa, 428, set up kingdom, 439
- Vandals of North Africa under Gaiseric sack Rome, 455
- Regime of "puppet emperors" in Italy, 455–476
- Last emperor of the West, Romulus Augustus, is deposed by Odoacer, 476
- Barbarian kings at Ravenna, 476–540

# CHAPTER 1

# The Roman Family at Home

## The Paterfamilias and Marriage

Within the Roman family, there is much greater intimacy between a husband and wife than in Greece, where men and women see relatively little of each other. To the Romans, the concept of family is very important—it is the cornerstone of society.

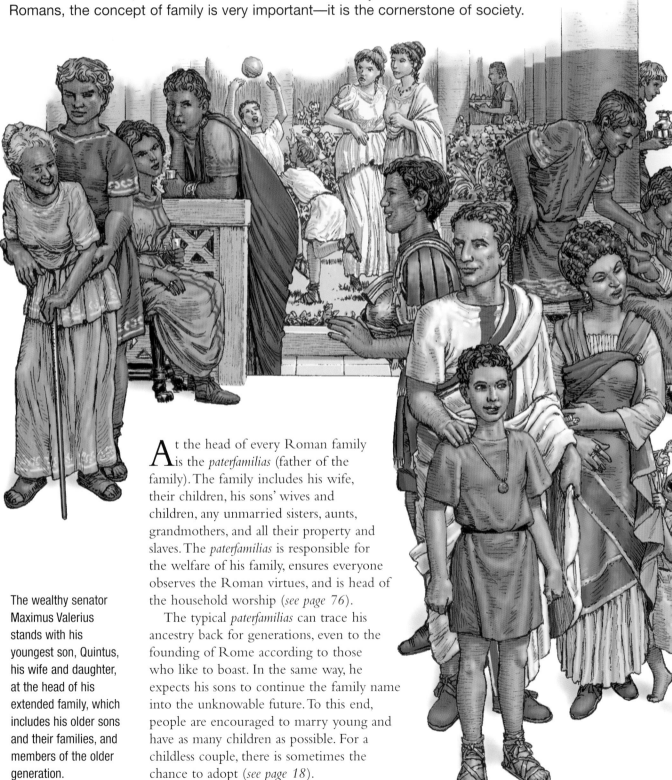

The wealthy senator Maximus Valerius stands with his youngest son, Quintus, his wife and daughter, at the head of his extended family, which includes his older sons and their families, and members of the older generation.

At the head of every Roman family is the *paterfamilias* (father of the family). The family includes his wife, their children, his sons' wives and children, any unmarried sisters, aunts, grandmothers, and all their property and slaves. The *paterfamilias* is responsible for the welfare of his family, ensures everyone observes the Roman virtues, and is head of the household worship (*see page 76*).

The typical *paterfamilias* can trace his ancestry back for generations, even to the founding of Rome according to those who like to boast. In the same way, he expects his sons to continue the family name into the unknowable future. To this end, people are encouraged to marry young and have as many children as possible. For a childless couple, there is sometimes the chance to adopt (*see page 18*).

## Getting engaged to be married

Marriages are usually arranged between families for business, political, or social reasons—the feelings of the young couple for each other are rarely taken into account. Although in theory the wife is subject to her husband's will, in practice Roman matrons exercise great influence over the household and have their say over a child's future spouse. Girls may be betrothed at birth and allowed to marry at the age of 12, but most wait until they are 14.

The financial arrangement between husband and wife depends on the marriage contract made. In some cases the bride's money will become the property of her husband's father, but in imperial times this is rarer and women often retain control of their own belongings.

A feast is held to mark the betrothal, and the marriage contract agreed between the two fathers and written out. On the night before the wedding, the bride offers all her childhood toys and belongings to the gods at the household shrine (*see also page 76*).

## The wedding ceremony

Wedding days must be carefully chosen to avoid the many unlucky days in the Roman calendar (*see pages 40–41*). The bride's house is decorated with garlands of flowers and colored ribbons. When the guests arrive, a priest takes the "auspices" and asks the gods if the day is favorable. The bride wears a white tunic and a vivid orange veil over her traditionally braided hair.

After the fathers-in-law have signed the contract, the chief bridesmaid takes the bride's hand and joins it with the groom's. He places a ring on the third finger of the bride's left hand, over which she pledges her loyalty to him and promises to follow him in all things.

After the ceremony, it is customary for the families and their guests to enjoy a feast at the house of the bride's father before the newlyweds lead a procession to the groom's home. Torch-bearers light the way and flutists play cheery music. When they arrive, the bride smears the doorposts with fat and oil, and adds wreaths of wool. Then her husband lifts her up and carries her over the threshold in an act of ritual abduction (*see "The Sabine Women"*).

## Roman divorce

In early Rome, divorce was rare and only happened if the husband desired it. By the end of the Republic, divorces had become more frequent among the patricians and wealthier equestrian class of citizen.

In the imperial period anyone—husband or wife—may divorce without giving a reason, so long as he or she shouts, "I divorce you!" three times in front of a citizen acting as a witness.

The bridegroom carries his new wife across the threshold of his home, a tradition dating back to Rome's earliest days when the largely male settlement stole women from the neighboring Sabine tribe.

### The Sabine Women

In legend, Romulus broke away from others of his tribe and, with a band of outcasts, founded Rome on the Palatine Hill. He became concerned that there were insufficient women to ensure the survival of the new state, so he arranged a feast for the neighboring tribe of Sabines, who lived on the Quirinal Hill, the most northerly of the seven hills of Rome.

The "Romans" plied the Sabine men with alcohol, and when they were thoroughly drunk, Romulus and his supporters seized their wives and daughters. Fortunately, the women fell in love with their captors and ultimately forced their men to make peace between Romans and Sabines.

# Children in the Roman Home

Most parents take their responsibilities very seriously and try to make sure their children grow up to be respectful sons and daughters—model citizens of the future.

To the proud father, the infant son cradled in his arm is the prospect of a bright future for the family clan. This figure is from a sarcophagus.

Rome's first emperor, Caesar Augustus, who encouraged his citizens to have many children, only had a daughter by his first marriage. He became the stepfather of his second wife's two sons by her first marriage. Sadly, the elder, named Drusus, died early, leaving Tiberius (below), who Augustus did not like.

### Fact box

Emperor Augustus adopted no less than five "sons" in his efforts to obtain an heir. Only one—his stepson Tiberius—survived to become emperor after him.

After her marriage, the teenaged wife looks forward to having children with some fear—and for good reason. Childbirth is a dangerous process, the infant death rate is high (as many as one in every three), and many unfortunate girls die while giving birth through the lack of proper medical care.

Although the parents want to see their sons and daughters having lots of offspring, most families must be content with two or three children—among which ideally there should be at least one son.

In a family where no male heir arrives, it is customary to adopt one. This might be either from near or distant relatives who are not capable of providing for their son, or from another family lucky to have several boys, and for whom an alliance will be socially useful. The adopted son takes his adoptive father's name and receives all the rights that a natural son would enjoy.

### The naming day

Soon after the successful birth of a son, the proud father takes the baby in his arms and lifts him up before the members of the household to prove his paternal bond. A few days later comes an occasion almost as important as the birth—the *dies lustricus*, or naming day. The custom of handing down names to children is of great significance to Romans.

A boy's name is normally composed of three parts. The *praenomen* (given name), *nomen* (family name, referring to the *gens*, or clan), and *cognomen* (nickname, although it means more and often describes the particular branch of the family, *see "Naming conventions"*). Girls are not usually distinguished by a *cognomen*, and often take the *praenomina* of their fathers or mothers, even if three girls should end up with identical names. When that happens, the eldest is referred to as *Major*, the younger as *Minor*, and—if there is a third—she is called *Tertia*, which means "Third."

Many days mother is happy to leave the care of the baby to a maid.

Unruly boys are never far from the wrath of their stern father.

## How Romans are named

Romans rarely spell out a person's full name. It is not necessary because not many first names or *praenomenina* are used. Since everyone knows them, they are written as only the capital letter or an abbreviation. This list contains the most popular names.

| | | | | | |
|---|---|---|---|---|---|
| A. | = | Aulus | N. | = | Numerius |
| App. | = | Appius | P. | = | Publius |
| D. | = | Decimus | Q. | = | Quintus |
| C. | = | Gaius | Ser. | = | Servius |
| Cn. | = | Gnaeus | Sex. | = | Sextus |
| K. | = | Kaeso | Sp. | = | Spurius |
| L. | = | Lucius | Ti. | = | Tiberius |
| M. | = | Marcus | T. | = | Titus |

There are more nicknames, or *cognomina* in use. This is useful because if only *praenomina* were used people would get confused as to whom anyone was referring! These range from honorifics voted for military victories, such as "Africanus," to personal characteristics. Latin is a robust language and some *cognomina* are unflattering—rude, sarcastic, or witty. The list on the right contains some common nicknames.

| Latin | English | Latin | English |
|---|---|---|---|
| Africanus | conqueror of Africa | Mactator | butcher |
| Agelastus | never smiles | Magnus | great |
| Ahenobarbus | bronze (red)-bearded | Maximus | greatest |
| Albinus | white-skinned or pale | Metellus | a mercenary |
| Bestia | a beast | Mus | mouse |
| Britannicus | conqueror of Britain | Nasica | nosy |
| Brocchus | buck-toothed | Nepos | grandfather |
| Brutus | animal stupidity | Nerva | stringy, or tough |
| Caecus | blind | Piso | I grind down |
| Caepio | onion seller | Pius | loyal son |
| Caesar | fine head of hair | Porcella | piglet |
| Calvus | bald | Postumus | born after father's death |
| Caprarius | a goat | Ravilla | talked himself hoarse |
| Carbo | a cinder, burned out | Rufus | red-haired |
| Cato | shrewd/highly strung | Ruso | country bumpkin |
| Catulus | pup, or cub | Scaevola | left-handed |
| Cicero | chickpea | Scaurus | swollen feet |
| Cotta | splash of wine | Scipio | a ceremonial rod |
| Crassus | thick | Silanus | ugly flat face |
| Cunctator | one who holds back | Silo | flat-nosed |
| Dives | heavenly | Strabo | cross-eyed |
| Flaccus | big ears | Tubero | hump-backed, or |
| Galba | potbelly | | immoral |
| Germanicus | conqueror of Germany | Varro | bandy-legged |
| Lentulus | tardy, or slow | Vatia | knock-kneed |
| Lepidus | wonderful man | Verrucosis | wart-covered |

After the joyous naming ceremony, the father hangs a good-luck charm, known as a *bulla*, around the child's neck. This will ward off the *numina* (evil spirits) and is worn throughout childhood. Boys only give up their *bulla* when they take up the toga of manhood (*see pages 42–43*), girls on their wedding day.

## Early education

Until it is time for serious education to begin, young children are looked after by their mothers, or by a household slave girl. For boys, games such as blindman's buff, leapfrog, and knuckle-bones are popular. Children build toy houses, use whips and spinning tops, roll hoops, and play on swings. Rag and clay dolls are favorites with girls.

For boys, schooling might begin at home, under father's stern eye or under the tutelage of a *litterator*, a hired slave to act as a teacher. But by the time they reach the age of seven, education begins in earnest.

**Above:** A child's good-luck charm: the *bulla*.

Tired of their dolls, these girls play an energetic game of ball.

The boys are intent on a bout of knuckle-bones, like the ones seen here.

# Education for the Wealthy and the Middle Classes

Among the privileged classes, both boys and girls go to schools of their own, although for girls the education is more basic and ends at around the age of 12, when they might be expected to marry.

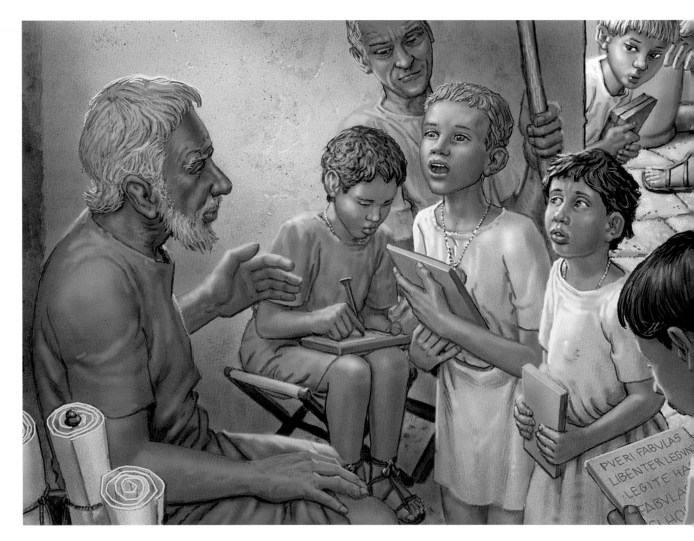

A new arrival takes a worried peek into the cramped classroom located at the rear of a grocery store. While some of the pupils scribble exercises on their tablets, one boy eagerly recites a poem his teacher has given him to memorize.

A girl concentrates on what she will need to know to become a good wife and mother. However, the ancient tradition of the Roman matron training to be like her Greek counterpart, sitting at home spinning and weaving, has largely disappeared.

The wealthy Roman wife has plenty of slaves to do her domestic chores, and plenty of stores selling clothes, bed linen, and furnishings. Therefore old, virtuous matronly skills are rarely learned. This allows for time for girls to concentrate on learning from a private tutor how to read and write.

Boys may also be tutored at home, but most are sent to a school once they are seven, where they have a harder time than their sisters at home. There is no public education system as in Greece. The Roman *ludus* or primary school is fee-paying, usually only a single room in a house, or a part of a shop curtained off from the street. The best *ludi magistri* or school masters are Greeks, who teach classes of up to 12 boys.

Lessons start with learning the alphabet, and to read and write in Latin and Greek. Exercises are done with a metal or bone stylus to write on a wooden tablet coated with wax. When the space is used up, the wax can be scraped off and a fresh layer quickly applied. Some tablets have several wooden "leaves," attached with cord on one edge, to make a sort of book.

...chool discipline is ...arsh. Stern fathers ...xpect the teacher ...o lay on the rod ...hen their sons ...isbehave.

## Secondary education

At about the age of 11, some boys go to a *grammaticus* (secondary or high school), where they learn philosophy, history, geography, higher mathematics, music, and astronomy. Romans respect the knowledge of the Greeks so learning Greek is an important part of the *grammaticus* curriculum.

One purpose of secondary education is to prepare the student for study with a teacher of public speaking called a *rhetor*. The sons of senators, state officials, or senior military men start this training for their future political life at about the age of 14.

## Speak up or be ignored

Anyone who wants to become a politician or a lawyer must be able to speak well in public, otherwise they will remain unnoticed…and unelected to office. The very wealthy send their sons to Athens to learn from the best Greek teachers in rhetoric (the art of speaking in public).

Training in rhetoric can take many years—the famous orator Cicero continued his studies until he was almost 30. But the expense of secondary education means few poor people become politicians or lawyers.

Children of the poorest citizens may not receive any education at all, because their parents need them to go out to work as soon as they are able. The best will become apprenticed to craftsmen, but the laziest will become part of the "mob," the rabble that throngs Rome's streets, fed by the corn dole (*see page 31, "Food for the poor"*).

The young man who either fails in his rhetoric lessons or whose family lacks the money to educate him will end up as part of the Roman mob.

The writing stylus has a flat scraper at one ...nd for erasing small errors. When an exercise ...s finished and checked by the teacher, the ...upil can erase the whole work by ...viping a warmed cloth over the wax ...urface, making it ready to use again.

Discipline is harsh, and slackers ...isk frequent thrashings with the cane, leather ...hong, or eel-skin strap. Fathers expect no less ...f the hired teacher—endurance of pain is ...ood training for the future soldiers of the ...mpire. Richer families send a specialized ...ervant called a *litterator* along to the *ludus* ...vith the boy, to make sure he behaves well ...nd applies himself to his lessons. The *litterator* ...an also apply the rod if his pupil slacks.

**Left:** Wax tablets are used for taking notes, quick dictation, or military messages. For writing on paper or parchment, ink and pens of sharpened reed are used.

# Roman Books and Literature

Although Romans up to the mid-Republican era regarded literary writing with suspicion as an effeminately Greek habit, they soon threw caution to the wind and have since made up for lost time with an outpouring of great poetry and prose.

Educated Romans are fond of reading, and most cities have numerous publishers and book stores supplying wealthy individuals' private shelves. Larger temples and public baths often contain libraries, usually one for Greek books and one for Latin. The books are long scrolls made from papyrus in the Egyptian method (*see "Paper-making"*). In some cases, parchment made from washed animal skins is used, but its weight makes a scroll cumbersome and heavy.

Books take a long time to produce, because each copy is written out by hand. A publisher's workshop is a busy place, filled by scribes—usually Greek slaves—making endless copies of an author's original script. The text is written in columns, working from left to right along the length of the scroll. This might be as much as 30 feet in length. Completed scrolls are kept in leather caskets.

The copying process is one of mass production. In each work group of anything between three or four to as many as ten scribes, a hired man sits and reads aloud the author's text. The scribes then take down the dictation. When there is a rush job to be done, scribes work in shifts throughout the night, but the copying can often become sloppy, resulting in furious authors threatening to take their work elsewhere.

### Rome's famous writers

Roman authors are famous for prose stories, poetry, histories, plays, military handbooks and memoirs, and satires. Julius Caesar's *Commentaries* are memoirs about the Gallic and Civil Wars, but he is known for other books, including one on jokes.

Quintus Horatius Flaccus (Horace, 65–8 BCE) is Rome's greatest poet and satirist. Decimus Junius Juvenalis (Juvenal, c.50/70–127 CE) is known for his satires on

Finished book scrolls are kept in a leather book casket.

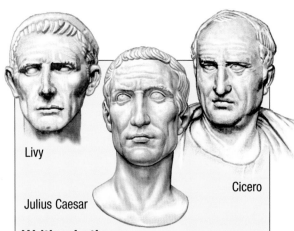

Livy

Julius Caesar

Cicero

Scene in a busy Roman publishing house, where the mass production of an author's books is taking place. While one man reads from the author's original, a team of scribes copies the text on papyrus scrolls. They may have to repeat the process several times for a book in popular demand.

the follies of Roman society. Titus Livius (Livy, c.59 BCE–17 CE) is regarded as the first authoritative Roman historian.

Publius Ovidius Naso (Ovid, 43 BCE–17 CE) was a prolific poet whose rudeness resulted in his banishment by Augustus. Titus Petronius Niger (Petronius the Arbiter, 27 BCE–66 CE)—another irreverent writer—is famous for his *Satyricon*, a tale of disreputable youths, vulgar wealth, and over-eating.

Gaius Suetonius Tranquillus (c.70–140 CE) is a lawyer and author of the biographies of Julius Caesar and the first 11 emperors, from Augustus to Domitian. Gaius Cornelius Tacitus (c.56–117 CE) is another historian of the same period, best known for his work about his father-in-law Agrippa's campaigns in Britain.

## Writing Latin

The Latin alphabet was generally used throughout the Roman Empire, although it coexisted with Greek in the East. It consisted of 23 letters and later in the Middle Ages the Roman "I" was split into i and j; and their "V" became u, v, and w. In this way, Romans spelled Julius Caesar as IVLIVS CAESAR. Through the later influence of the Christian Church, Latin became the common language of Western civilization among educated people.

## Surviving fragments

Roman authors wrote on papyrus or waxed tablets, only fragments of which have survived the centuries. This means that most authors' works in Latin today are the result of copying during the medieval period, and of course much remains lost. Those who wrote more in Greek have survived better, because the climate in the East was better suited to preserving papyrus manuscripts.

## Paper-making

The Romans import great quantities of Egyptian papyrus reed for making paper. The outer fibers of the reed are peeled away and the core of the stalk sliced into very thin strips (**A**). These are then soaked in water to remove the sugar content, pounded, the excess water removed, and placed side by side in rows, slightly overlapping.

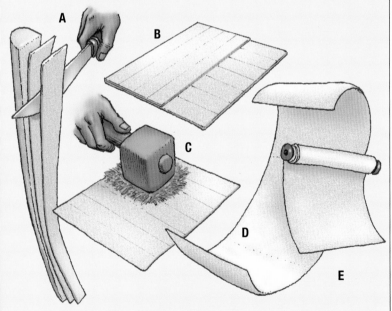

A second set of strips is placed above the first at right angles and the starch from the strips glues them together (**B**). After a further pounding, the raw papyrus sheet is left to dry out for about six days (**C**). After drying the sheet's surface is polished to a smooth finish with a shell or piece of smooth ivory. Single sheets are then glued together to form a longer sheet (**D**). In the best quality papyrus, the joins are barely noticeable. Wood or ivory rollers are fitted to either end of the scroll to make it easier to handle (**E**).

## Fact box

The first true books appear in the 4th century. Called a *codex*, instead of a long, single scroll, smaller pages are secured along one edge to make separate pages. The result is a book that can contain more information than a scroll, and is easier to carry around and read. *Codices* are also more convenient for storage on library shelves.

# Medicine, Illness, and Death

Most Roman medical knowledge has come from the Greeks, particularly the teachings of Greek healer Hippocrates. However, doctors still rely on religious rituals as well as their scientific treatments.

There is a powerful belief that the gods can help heal a sick person, particularly Aesculapius, the god of healing (this is the Roman spelling of the Greek god Asclepius). There are temples to Aesculapius throughout the Roman world. As do the Greeks, sick people spend a night in the temple, believing that their dreams will tell them how to cure their illnesses.

Army surgeons receive the most training in dealing with serious injuries to soldiers.

bone lever

hooks

## A scientific study

Those doctors who prefer to follow the example of Hippocrates tend to look at the natural, rather than the supernatural, world for cures. There are several great books written on the subject of herbal remedies. One of these books, *De Materia Medica*, was written by a Greek physician named Discorides, an army doctor. It catalogs almost 600 plants and over a hundred drugs he had tested on his patients. Doctors like Discorides believe that

## Romans follow Greek beliefs

If medical science fails the patient and death occurs, a sacred funeral ritual begins. Romans share some customs with the Greeks, such as placing a coin under the deceased's tongue to pay the ferryman to row the soul across the Styx to the underworld. There, the spirit will be judged and, depending on the verdict, sent on to Elysium (heaven) or Tartarus (hell).

Romans are also very practical and follow the Greek rituals just in case they might help, even though few Romans really believe in an afterlife in any heaven or hell. They think the soul exists only while family and friends remember them. This is why ancestor worship is such an important part of daily life (*see pages 76–77*).

When a rich person dies, their body is washed and rubbed with costly oil. It is then laid in state at home, covered by flowers and wreaths, and surrounded by candles and lamps, so that the family, clients (*see pages 44–45*), and friends may pay their respects.

## Funerals, burial, and cremation

On the day of the *pompa* or funeral procession the body is placed on a litter and carried by household slaves to the Forum accompanied by mourners. In the Forum a speech is made, usually by the eldest son, in praise of his father. From here, the procession makes its way to the prepared grave.

By ancient law, this must be outside the city's *pomerium*, the sacred boundary. So many of the main roads leaving Rome are lined with tombs, ranging from the modest to the magnificent, sometimes for more than

Many cemeteries have grown up along the major roads just outside city gates. These are prime spots and cost a great deal. Many fine mausoleums line the Appian Way for several miles. Slaves and the poor are buried with little or no ceremony in the city necropolis (cemetery), although most workers belong to a "funeral club" to which they pay a part of their salary in order to obtain a good funeral when their time comes.

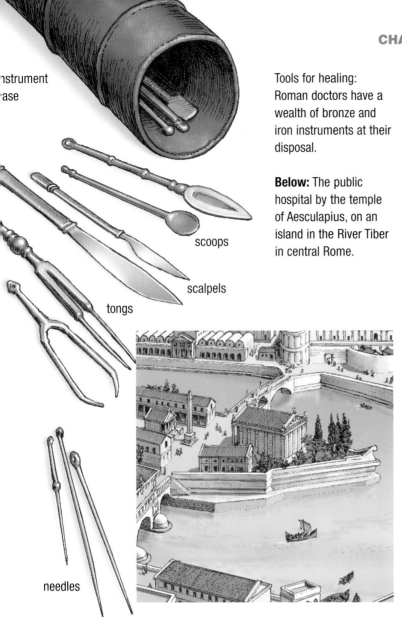

instrument case

scoops

scalpels

tongs

needles

Tools for healing: Roman doctors have a wealth of bronze and iron instruments at their disposal.

**Below:** The public hospital by the temple of Aesculapius, on an island in the River Tiber in central Rome.

what people eat plays an important part in how they feel, and advise their patients to alter their diets. They recommend regular exercise, fresh air, and visits to the many great public baths (*see pages 90–93*).

Army doctors also make the best surgeons, because they have so much opportunity to study human anatomy when attempting to repair the damage done to soldiers in battle. Scalpels, forceps, hooks, scoops, needles, and tongs make up their surgical kits. Unfortunately, the appalling pain suffered during major operations and amputations generally kills the patient.

## Free hospital treatment

The richest Romans have personal physicians to look after their families. Wealthy people can afford to pay a doctor to visit them at home, but the common folk must attend a surgery or hospital. Here, they are looked after by a number of doctors who are exempt from tax. In return, while they can accept fees, they must treat the poor free of charge.

The first public hospital started life as the Temple of Aesculapius on an island in the River Tiber. It was used to house elderly or disabled slaves who could no longer work. During the reign of Emperor Claudius, the temple became a hospital for the poor.

a mile. For the very poor and convicted criminals, there is a public cemetery beyond the Esquiline Hill.

In older times, Romans buried their dead, often placing the body in a stone coffin called a *sarcophagus*, but now cremation is preferred. For a simple ceremony, a pit is dug and filled with wood, over which the body is placed for burning, When the flames have died down, the ashes are covered with earth, and later a small headstone might be erected.

For the wealthy, elaborate ceremonies take place around a large fire known as a pyre. Relatives throw food and clothes onto the blaze. Later, the ashes are collected in a special funerary urn, which might be placed in the family's mausoleum or in an underground chamber called a *columbarium*, shared with many other families.

# A Roman Domus

As you walk along a street in Rome, it seems that there are no houses, only small shops lining its edges. This is because most better off homes rent the front rooms to tradespeople. Behind the shops, the luxury begins.

Most Romans live packed tightly together, like sardines in cans, in apartment blocks called *insulae* (*see pages 34–35*). Only very wealthy people can afford a *domus* or private house. The statistics prove the point—one survey shows 1790 private houses to 46,602 apartment blocks in Rome.

## Inside a wealthy *domus*

The typical *domus* is built on one floor. Although a few houses boast a second level, this is usually confined to one or two rooms, perhaps a study for the *paterfamilias*. A Roman home is much more sturdily built than a Greek house, using fired clay bricks secured by mortar, as shown on page 52.

The tiled or stone-slab flooring is often laid over a depth of concrete, a construction that allows for cellars underneath (although some districts of Rome are prone to flooding). The wealthiest houses—especially in the colder northern provinces—boast an underfloor central heating system called a *hypocaust* (*see pages 90 and 92*).

The family rooms are kept separate from the public areas, such as the *atrium*, where the *paterfamilias* greets his clients each workday morning. There is unlikely to be a *balneum* or bathroom, because the custom is to use the many smaller and monumental public baths every day.

**1.** The janitor greets a caller at the front door. Beyond, the *vestibula* leads to the *atrium*.

**2.** Rooms at the front, open to the street, are rented out as shops or *caupona* (taverns).

**3.** Guests are received in the *atrium*, an area open to the sky. The roof slopes down to an opening called the *compluvium*, which can be covered with canvas in cold weather. Rainwater is collected in a small pool, the *impluvium*. The water can be piped to a cistern in the cellar if it rises too high.

**4.** The family living rooms are located around the *atrium* and on the upper floor.

**5.** The dining room is called a *triclinium* because it contains three reclining couches for diners (*see pages 30–31*).

**6.** The *paterfamilias* has his *tablinum* (study) in the back, overlooking the garden.

**7.** The kitchen and latrine (*see pages 32–33*). Steps rise to the slave quarters.

**8.** Toward the rear of the *domus* is the *peristylium*, a walled garden planted with decorative trees and shrubs, and sometimes vegetables.

**9.** A shrine called a *lararium* houses the household gods and ancestor busts (*see page 76*).

**Fact box**

Keen gardeners, the Romans love
roses. Their petals are used in
wine-making, and dried rose petals
are used for powdering the body. In
the south of Italy, rose petals are
used for stuffing mattresses—
hence the saying "a bed of roses."

# The Matron's Role and Slaves

It is not thought appropriate for a rich matron to go out to work—her function is to run the household and direct the slaves. Just as is the case everywhere in the empire, at home nothing happens without slaves.

Poorer women who need to earn a wage often work in the markets, serve in stores, do needlework, or work as bath attendants. Because Roman women have much more independence than their Greek counterparts, some women below the wealthy senatorial and equestrian classes run their own businesses, such as laundries, cloth-making factories, perfumeries, or—at the other end of the smell scale—leather tanneries, which utilize urine from the *foricae* (public lavatories) in the tanning process.

Poor women must work to support themselves and their families.

## Organizing the slaves

However, the wealthy matron has an altogether more comfortable life. She directs the work of the household slaves, organizes the running of the home—and is expected to have children.

In general, slaves working in rich homes lead a relatively comfortable existence and are even treated affectionately by the families they serve. Greek slaves are considered to be the smartest and so they are the most expensive to buy. They work as doctors, tutors to the children, and secretaries to the *paterfamilias*. Other slaves work as butlers, hairdressers, personal maids, serving girls and boys, and cooks.

Loyal service can even lead to their master granting them their freedom, a process called *manumission*. A freed male slave usually remains associated with his former master as a client (*see pages 44–45*).

Two levels of Trajan's market surrounding his forum. The uppermost levels date from the Renaissance of the 14–15th centuries CE.

## A visit to the market

The matron goes out to do her shopping accompanied by a maid and a male slave as protector. Her shopping includes ready-made clothes or cloth for her slaves to make up the family's clothing needs, food, and luxury goods.

Around the Roman Forum there are numerous small *macella* (markets). A *macellum* was originally a meat market, but the term now covers any market hall housing shops and stalls selling such provisions as fruit, vegetables, pork, beef, fish, and solid wares such as pottery, jewelry, furniture, and other household goods.

The largest is Trajan's Market, a vast, purpose-built shopping mall on several levels, with over 150 individual shop units, many boasting handsome marble fronts. Here you can buy almost anything imaginable, from Greek antiques to wild animals for the arena, from expensive leather goods to oriental lamp stands.

The shopkeepers' slaves will deliver whatever goods the matron's own servants cannot carry home with them. The household butler, or major-domo, is responsible for seeing to their safe delivery and replacement of any damaged items.

On a busy shopping day, the household slaves are laden down with goods.

## The unlucky slave

Slaves in towns fare much better than those who are put to work in the fields, where the work is unrelenting. Lashings from their overseers are the norm, driven on by the bailiffs who manage the huge senatorial estates, called *latifundia*. On the farm, profit is everything, and field slaves are cheap labor, easily replaced when they fall dead over their hoes.

Worse still is the fate of slaves sent to work in mines digging out lead, iron, sulphur, copper, and silver. Barely fed and watered, living for months out of the sight of sun or sky, these slaves are nothing more than human digging machines. A mine slave's life is brutal and short; they are literally worked to death.

# Daily Roman Meals

While the poor are sustained chiefly by bread and a wheatmeal porridge known as *puls*, with meat a rare luxury, the rich of imperial Rome have turned dining into something like an artform.

The Romans in general eat three meals a day. Breakfast and lunch are very light for most people, from everyday citizens to the wealthy. The very poor might be glad to enjoy even one meal a day, which for the most part consists of cereal in the form of bread or *puls* (porridge), occasionally supplemented by vegetables or a little meat.

*Ientaculum* (breakfast) is usually simply bread dipped in watered-down wine. Sometimes a little honey is used, and perhaps a few dates or olives might be added. *Prandium* (lunch) is a similar meal of bread, or leftovers from the previous day's main meal. Many Romans skip their *prandium* altogether.

*Cena* (dinner) is the main meal of the day, generally served in the late afternoon when everyone has returned from the baths. For the lower classes, *cena* is a simple meal of vegetables with olive oil, but the well-to-do enjoy elaborate feasts consisting of three courses called *ab ovo usque ad mala* (from the egg to the apples).

## An elaborate dinner

The first course, known as *gustus*, consists of such appetizers as salads, radishes, eggs, mushrooms, oysters and other shellfish, and sardines. It is followed by a drink of *mulsum* (wine sweetened with honey).

The main course, known as *lena* or *prima mensa* (main table) might contain as many as seven dishes, including pork, poultry, fish, game, and exotic birds. These are served with sauces and vegetables.

The final course is the *secunda mensa* (second table), so called because rather than clear the dishes of the first two courses, the slaves remove the table and replace it with another one. This course offers fruit (plain, stuffed and in sauces), honey cakes, and nuts.

The food is served with plenty of wine, from a choice of more than 200 varieties from all over the empire.

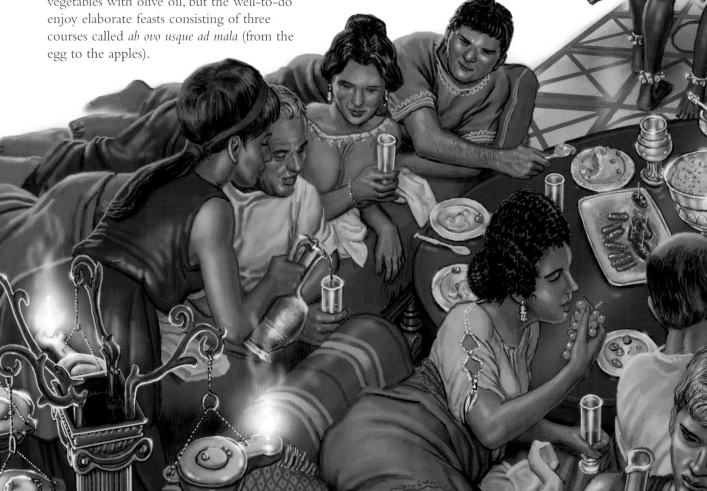

## The *triclinium*

The dining room of a Roman house is called the *triclinium* because traditionally it houses three reclining couches for the diners, arranged around a low, centrally placed table. At formal banquets, each couch seats three guests, although the *paterfamilias* might allow more of his family to crowd in at a family dinner. In very rich homes, the *triclinium* may be very large and have room for two or more sets of couches and tables.

In early Republican times, only men reclined to eat. The household's women sat opposite the men on chairs, but in the imperial period both men and women share the couches. The three couches are named *summus*, *medius*, and *imus* (top, middle, and bottom). Diners are seated according to their social status, with the most honored guest seated at *medius 3*. The host often sits next to him at *imus 1*.

Romans do not use knives or forks. Most dishes are eaten with the fingers, or sometimes with spoons for sauces. Slaves are on hand to wash greasy hands with rose-petal water and dry them on soft cloths.

## Waited on hand and foot

Banquets commonly last for several hours, with acrobats, dancers, poets, and musicians offering entertainment between courses. Slaves take care of the guests' every need—removing their shoes and replacing them with sandals, waving off flies with peacock-feather fans, washing guests' hands with perfumed water, and serving the food. It is customary to have only the most handsome slaves to cut up and serve the food or pour the wine.

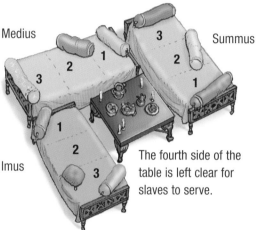

Medius — Summus

Imus

The fourth side of the table is left clear for slaves to serve.

## Food for the poor

The poor in the countryside have access to a wider variety of food than the urban lower classes. Rome is crowded, housing poor, and unemployment widespread. To prevent continual rioting, the state subsidizes grain prices and even gives it away free to very poor registered citizens on a monthly basis, a system known as the corn dole.

Since almost everyone lives in rented accommodation in an *insula* apartment which has no cooking facilities, people have to take their wheat to the local *pistor* (baker), who bakes their loaves for them. Other hot and cold food can be purchased from the many local food shops and taverns (*see* pages 46–47)

# In the Kitchen of a Wealthy Domus

A senator expects to hold many dinner parties for important guests, and wants to display his wealth by serving luxurious meals. His kitchen, therefore, is large and well equipped.

The Roman cook has a wide variety of cooking utensils. Unlike the elaborate glass, metal, and pottery utensils used in the *triclinium* for serving meals, cooking pots are simply and strongly constructed to stand up to continual use and temperature changes.

The kitchen has several stoves. A large brick-built stove is used for cooking food in bronze or earthenware pots over charcoal. The pots—some open, some with close-fitting lids—are placed on metal tripods or pottery stands so that they do not rest directly on the fire, which might cause them to crack.

A fireplace burning a mixture of wood and charcoal and fitted with a rotating spit is used for roasting larger cuts of meat. Whole pigs or large birds can be cooked in this manner. A portable earthenware oven fired by charcoal is used for baking bread, pastries, and cakes.

## The luxury of fresh water

Since this house is connected to the public water supply, the kitchen slaves have the luxury of fresh water for cleaning fruit and vegetables, as well as cleaning pots, pans and knives. However, the latrine next to the kitchen, making use of the running water, is really only reserved for family use; the slaves must make do with the nearest public latrine.

A collection of *amphorae* and jugs sits in one corner awaiting use. The jugs have thick sides and narrow necks with small openings to keep liquids cool in the summer heat. Beside them are sacks containing ground wheat, chickpeas, and such dried fruits as dates and grapes.

Although the cook has a variety of herbal flavorings available, the most popular Roman seasoning is *liquamen*, also called *garum*. Made by allowing fish entrails and small whole fish to rot and ferment in salted vats under the sun for anything up to three months, *garum* sounds horrible, but it goes into many dishes, including desserts.

This busy kitchen has the benefit of running water from the public supply, useful for washing up—and for flushing the home's adjacent latrine.

A portable earthenware oven.

A cooking pot sits on an iron stand to avoid direct contact with flaming charcoal.

**Below:** Commonly used pottery vessels.

### Fact box

Roman food had little in common with modern Italian food. Rice, pasta, and tomatoes were not yet known, and Romans had little liking for garlic.

**1.** Woodburning braziers are the only form of heating, but they are a great fire risk, and there are no chimneys.

**2.** *Insulae* have no internal drains, so people throw waste into the streets below.

**3.** Rich people can afford comfortable apartments with many rooms. These are on a lower floor of the building.

**4.** Few apartments in an *insula* have their own bathrooms. People use the public baths and latrines (*see pages 90–93*).

**5.** Wealthy homes are often connected to the public water supply (*see pages 74–75*), but there is no running water in the *insula*. Instead, people fetch their water from the many public fountains.

**6.** Rooms at street level are rented out by the landlord for use as shops or *caupona* (taverns).

**7.** A narrow staircase connects the different floor levels.

# High-Rise Living

Unlike the strictly ordered provincial towns and cities, Rome has expanded over the centuries without any town planning. To create living space in the cramped area, most apartments rise to several stories.

The majority of Rome's population is housed in rented rooms packed into *insulae* (apartment blocks or tenements) owned by a handful of wealthy landlords. Built around a courtyard, an *insula* has several floors raised above shops fronting the street.

Typically, *insulae* are of three or four stories. Emperor Augustus limited the height of *insulae* to a maximum of five floors, but unscrupulous landlords often get away with cheating, and in Rome's Subura district they might rise to six or seven floors.

## Unsafe and dangerous

*Insulae* have a reputation for being unsafe. Fire from cooking and woodburning braziers in winter is a continual hazard. *Insulae* are constructed from timber frames and cheap but perishable mud bricks, which means that they burn easily, and their height makes them prone to disastrous collapse. All too often the hapless victims of lower floors are buried under tons of burning debris.

In a better ordered town, such as Rome's port at Ostia, *insulae* (like the model of the one pictured below) are more soundly built from concrete and fired bricks. But they remain as cramped inside and lack the basic amenities a *domus* owner takes for granted, such as private toilets and running water.

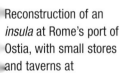
Reconstruction of an *insula* at Rome's port of Ostia, with small stores and taverns at street level.

## The *vigiles*

The fire service that Augustus created for Rome in about 27 BCE has seven brigades, called *vigiles* (watchmen), each with a thousand men and responsible for two of city's 14 districts. The districts are under the control of magistrates elected annually by lot. The districts are further divided into wards under locally elected supervisors.

The fire fighters use wheeled fire engines equipped with hand pumps, but they can only deliver a small quantity of water. Buckets and sponges are used to dampen undamaged walls to prevent the fire from spreading, but in most cases the blazing building has to be left to burn out, while adjacent ones are pulled down to make a fire-break.

Before Augustus created a permanent fire fighting service, unscrupulous businessmen often employed henchmen to hinder people trying to put out a fire. Once the building had crashed into cinders, the businessman stepped in and bought the lot for next to nothing. In this way, the rich grew richer, buying up whole quarters of the city.

# Roman Clothes and Fashion

Men and women's clothing is very similar, and fashions have changed very little over the centuries. Children tend to wear smaller versions of adult clothing.

The basic Roman garment is the tunic, knee-length for men, longer for women. The popular *stola* worn by the matron (front left) can be complemented by a *palla* (front right). The two men heading for a party (left) sport a fashionable *synthesis*. The senator and his son in the background are dressed in formal *togas*.

Most people wear clothes made from wool or linen, and garments are made from large uncut pieces of cloth. These are folded and pinned with pins called *fibulae*, or tied around the waist with belts. Tailors and clothing stores that sell ready-made garments do a little needlework, but clothes that need a lot of sewing are rare because the needles are made of bone and therefore clumsy.

Fine cotton cloth is imported from India and silk comes from the Far East via the traders of the eastern Mediterranean coast. Both are expensive, with silk costing three to four times its weight in gold.

## Men's clothes

The loincloth is the universal undergarment, which also acts as nightwear. Over a loincloth, a man wears a short-sleeved *tunica* (tunic), made from two rectangles stitched at the sides and belted around the waist. It extends from the shoulders to the knees.

Children and slaves commonly wear a tunic, but the senatorial and equestrian classes generally wear a *toga* over the tunic when out of doors. A senator's tunic has a broad purple stripe, and a member of the equestrian class has a narrow purple stripe, running from the shoulder to the hem, front and back.

Charioteers wear tunics dyed the color of their team (*see pages 84–85*).

In rural areas and the northern provinces, people wear cloaks, especially in winter. But the Celtic-style trousers are considered to be barbarian attire. In Rome, if it gets cold, men simply wear two or more tunics—although they never have long sleeves, which is considered to be effeminate.

## The toga

The *toga* is a heavy, awkward item of men's clothing, but the *toga* distinguishes a Roman citizen and so emperors insist on their being worn. They are of fine white wool, and require frequent cleaning by a fuller.

The *toga virilis* is a plain white and worn by all ordinary men. The *toga praetexta* (bordered toga) has a purple stripe and is worn by magistrates. Until the age of about 15 or 16, boys also wear the *toga praetexta*. A senator's *toga* has a broad purple stripe (*latus clavus*), while an equestrian's has a narrow purple stripe (*clavus angustus*). An emperor's *toga* is entirely purple. A *toga* made of pure black wool, called a *toga pulla*, is worn at funerals and by those in mourning.

In the country, men usually wear a more practical cloak over a tunic, and for formal evening meals a smart, loose gown called a *synthesis* is popular.

## Women's clothes

Women also wear loincloths (and sometimes breast bands) and tunics. Two-piece garments resembling a bikini are popular when taking exercise at the baths. Married women (matrons) wear a *stola* over the tunic, a long, full dress gathered up by a girdle, usually with a colored border around the neck.

The *palla* is a large rectangle of cloth that can be draped around the *stola* in many ways. Out of doors, women also wear a cloak.

## Footwear

Romans wear a wide variety of shoes— hobnailed boots, slippers, and sandals made from leather. Cobblers make ready-to-wear and made-to-measure shoes ranging from the plain *calcei* (heavy boot) to elegantly designed, open-weave ladies' sandals.

## Makeup

Women use various perfumes and facial cosmetics. A pale skin is always fashionable, and the face is whitened with powdered chalk or white lead.

Eyelids are darkened with ash or antimony (a dark-colored metal). Cheeks and lips are blushed and painted red by using the sediment of red wine, or a plant dye called *fucus*.

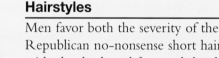

A toga is roughly semicircular in shape, about 18 ft in length by 7 ft deep. Drape the left-hand end over the left shoulder. Gather into a roll a large fold from the middle of the right-hand section and throw over the left shoulder. Take the rest of the left-hand section and pull it up under the front of the right-hand section.

## Hairstyles

Men favor both the severity of the Republican no-nonsense short hair cut, with closely shaved face, and the slightly longer dressed locks and full beard of imperial times. In any case, most mornings start with a visit to the *tonsor* (barber) for a shave and trim, or a clean-up.

Women have their hair done at home by slaves who style elaborate creations from their mistresses' hair, or by the addition of hairpieces and wigs. Wigs made from the blond hair of Germans captured in battle are very popular. The whole construction is held in place by a veritable scaffold of pins, combs, and braided hairnets.

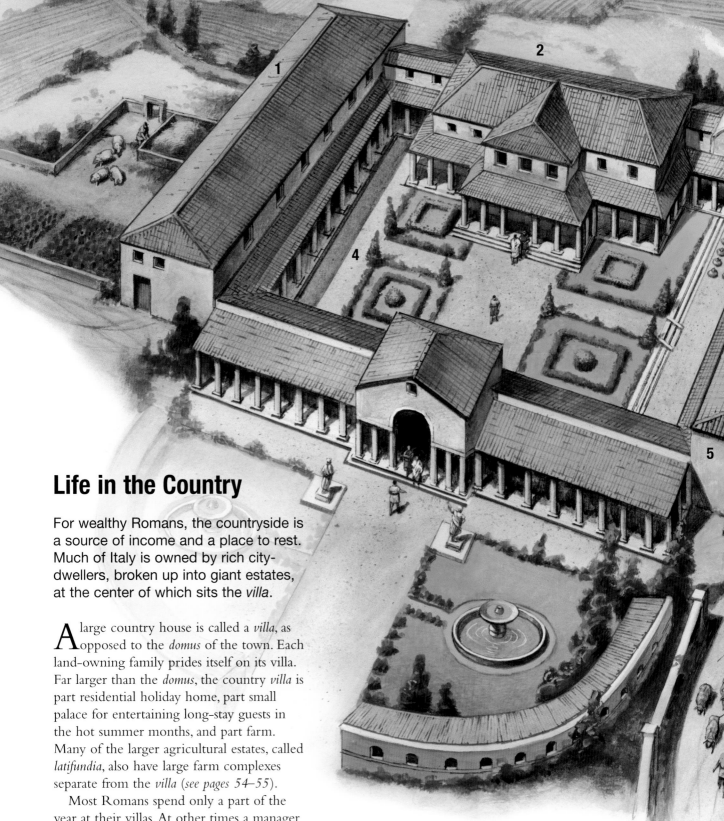

# Life in the Country

For wealthy Romans, the countryside is a source of income and a place to rest. Much of Italy is owned by rich city-dwellers, broken up into giant estates, at the center of which sits the *villa*.

A large country house is called a *villa*, as opposed to the *domus* of the town. Each land-owning family prides itself on its villa. Far larger than the *domus*, the country *villa* is part residential holiday home, part small palace for entertaining long-stay guests in the hot summer months, and part farm. Many of the larger agricultural estates, called *latifundia*, also have large farm complexes separate from the *villa* (*see pages 54–55*).

Most Romans spend only a part of the year at their villas. At other times a manager and a team of slaves run the estate. The typical country house is called a *peristyle villa*, a complex of buildings surrounding a large garden courtyard. The family and public rooms are lavishly decorated with mosaic floors and elaborately painted rural scenes on the walls. There is almost certainly a spacious bathhouse for the use of the family, their guests, and at times by the domestic workers.

**1.** The *villa urbana* is where the family lives when in residence. The rooms are very luxurious and may be heated by a *hypocaust* (*see page 92*), which also supplies hot water to the baths.

**2.** The public reception rooms take the place of the *atrium* of the *domus*. Here the master of the house can receive his clients, many of whom will travel for miles out of the city to visit.

**3.** Unlike the many rooms of the large public baths in Rome, the baths consist of a hot room and a simple cold plunge pool.

**4.** The garden colonnade faces onto the large formal gardens in front of the *villa*.

**5.** The working part of the villa is called the *villa rusticana*. It includes a cow shed, granary, grape-pressing and fermentation rooms, and accommodation for the farm overseer and his assistants. Slaves live in separate quarters nearby.

**Right:** Mosaic floors are an essential part of any aspiring Roman's home. Scenes of gods and heroes are suited to the city *domus*, but for a well-to-do rural *villa* images of wildlife are preferred.

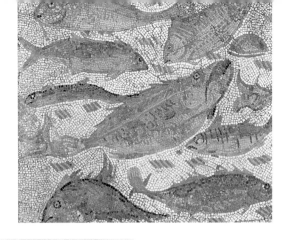

**Left:** Wall painting depicting a calm, quiet, rural scene—the very thing for a *villa*'s dining room to help the guests' digestion.

## A villa gone mad...

The most lavish *villa* ever built in Rome covered a ground area of 125 acres, all land cleared by the Emperor Nero after the Great Fire of 64 CE that damaged a great part of the city. Nero's villa stretched between the Palatine and Esquiline Hills, laid out like a country park, with a lake, woodlands and fields. Even the recently constructed platform for the Temple of Claudius was "stolen" to become a formal garden for the mad emperor.

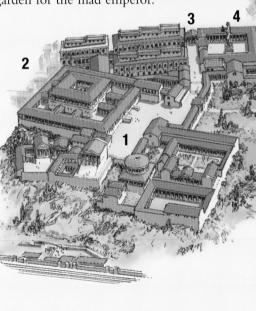

**7.** The Great Lake (where the Colosseum will be constructed after Nero's death).

**3.** The Sacred Way (Sacra Via).

**5.** Porticoes along the New Way (Nova Via).

**8.** The Golden House (Domus Aurea)

**1.** Nero's new palace on the Palatine Hill.

**2.** Eastern end of the Roman Forum.

**4.** Nero's colossal statue.

**6.** Temple of the Divine Claudius.

**9.** The Subura district.

# CHAPTER 2
# A Working Life

## Date and Time—Roman Punctuality

The Roman Empire runs on efficiency in everything. To this end, managing the calendar, dates, and the time of day is essential to the well-being of civilization.

Before Julius Caesar reformed the Roman calendar, it was the job of the priests to keep the human calendar in line with the solar year. Unfortunately, they were not very good at doing this, randomly adding "leap" days until the seasons were about 80 days out of kilter with the calendar months.

With the help of a Greek astronomer from Alexandria, Caesar corrected this in 46 BCE by making the year 445 days long, which made summer and winter where they should be. And then in the next January, he introduced a year of 365 days, divided into 12 months. To adjust for the extra quarter of a day in the solar year, Caesar allowed for a leap year by adding an extra day between February 23 and 24 on every fourth year.

The leap day, known as *bisextilis*, is not numbered, so to Romans it does not really exist. This makes it the unluckiest day in the Roman calendar, when no activity is permitted and all sensible Romans stay safely tucked up in their homes.

### The days in a month

The days (*dies* in Latin) are not numbered from the beginning of a month but from three special days called the Kalends (first of the month), the Nones (ninth day), and the Ides (13th day, or 15th in a month of 31 days). The Roman month is very organized and days are divided between four main types, with citizens told what activity may take place on each type of day.

On a *dies comitalis* citizens can vote on political matters. On a *dies fastus* the law courts operate and legal matters are handled, including marriages. On a *dies endotercisus* legal matters take place in the morning and voting in the afternoon. On a *dies nefastus* neither voting nor legal matters are allowed.

Market days (*dies nundinae*) occur every seven days, whatever its type unless it is

reserved for religious purposes. On market days agricultural produce is taken to markets. It is also a day for men of leisure to meet and exchange news in the Forum.

### Special days

In addition to the four basic types of day, there are days on which activity is restricted for religious reasons (*dies religiosi* or *feriae*, holidays), or prohibited altogether because they are unlucky. Such "black days" (*dies atri*) are not usually marked on calendars. They are tainted by the anniversaries of past disasters in war, when Romans remember and mourn the dead.

In the Roman year, a great many days are set aside for the major religious festivals (*see pages 80–81*). The chart below shows how the type of days work in the month of March, including festivals (in *italics*).

Sundials are simple to build, but suffer if the day is cloudy.

### The days of Martius (March) and festival days

| 1 | **Kalends**, *Matronalia\** | dies religiosus | 17 | *Agonalia* | dies religiosus |
|---|---|---|---|---|---|
| 2 | | dies fastus | 18 | | dies comitalis |
| 3 | | dies comitalis | 19 | *Quinquatria* | dies religiosus |
| 4 | | dies comitalis | 20 | *Quinquatria* | dies comitalis |
| 5 | | dies comitalis | 21 | *Quinquatria* | dies comitalis |
| 6 | | dies comitalis | 22 | *Quinquatria* | dies nefastus |
| 7 | **Nones** | dies fastus | 23 | *Tubilustrium\** | dies religiosus |
| 8 | | dies fastus | 24 | | dies fastus |
| 9 | | dies comitalis | 25 | | dies comitalis |
| 10 | | dies comitalis | 26 | | dies comitalis |
| 11 | | dies comitalis | 27 | | dies comitalis |
| 12 | | dies comitalis | 28 | | dies comitalis |
| 13 | | endotercisus | 29 | | dies comitalis |
| 14 | *Equirria\** | dies religiosus | 30 | | dies comitalis |
| 15 | **Ides**, *Anna Perenna\** | dies religiosus | 31 | *Luna* | dies comitalis |
| 16 | *Agonalia\** | dies fastus | | \* (see pages 80–81 for these festivals) | |

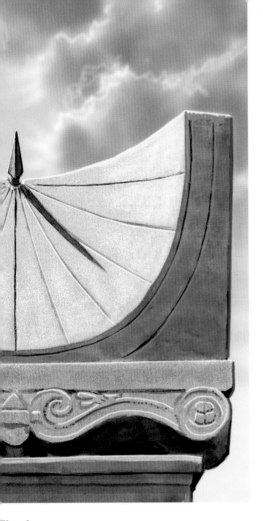

**Above:** A candle with carefully calibrated marks is an expensive and uncertain way of telling time. A glance at the sun's position is most people's guide.

**Below:** A public calendar.

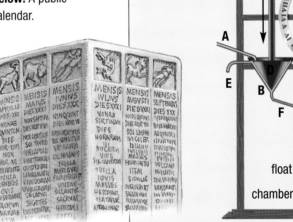

### Clocks or *horologia*

The shadow clock, or sundial (*solaria*) is is simple to build. However, it needs good sunlight, different scales depending on how north or south it is, and seasonal adjustment to account for the changing length of hours.

At home, people use candles calibrated by marks representing the hours. In theory, depending on the time of year, it should take an hour for the flame to burn down between two marks. In practice, they are very inaccurate. Hourglasses suffer from the same problem of constantly changing hour lengths during the year.

Water clocks, or *clepsydrae*, are more useful because they work at night as well, and seasonal adjustment is achieved by a clever mechanical system, as shown below.

A continuous supply of water enters the *clepsydra* by pipe **A**, filling the hollow cone **B**. By exerting pressure on lever **C**, solid cone **D** presses down on hollow cone **B**, restricting the water flow. Surplus water flows out through pipe **E**. Altering the pressure on the solid cone regulates the water flow through pipe **F** into the chamber. This alters the rate at which the float rises, and the rate at which the ratchet turns the clock's hand, accounting for unequal length of Roman hours.

### The hours

The day is divided into 12 night hours and 12 daylight hours. The first hour of the day is the hour after sunrise, and the 12th hour is the last hour before sunset. This means that the length of an hour continuously alters as the seasons move between summer and winter. In midwinter a daylight hour is about 45 minutes, and in midsummer 90 minutes.

Midnight and midday (*meridies*) are fixed at the sixth hour of night or day. Romans refer to the morning as *ante meridiem* (AM, before midday) and the afternoon as *post meridiem* (PM, after midday).

### Roman inclusive counting system

Romans count dates inclusively. This example, where we say "Let's meet on the third day from today…" shows how it works.

| Modern | today | tomorrow | | meet |
|---|---|---|---|---|
| | | 1st day | 2nd day | 3rd day |
| Roman (inclusive) | today 1st day | tomorrow 2nd day | *meet* 3rd day | |

### Fact box

The calendar reform introduced by Julius Caesar is called the Julian Calendar. This reform lasted until 1582, when Pope Gregory XIII made a slight adjustment to the calendar to its current form (he ordained that three days be left out in leap years every 400 years).

### Fact box

Weddings often take place in June, which is considered to be a particularly lucky month because of the number of public festivals held.

# Coming of Age

A young man's first shave is a religious occasion. It marks his approach to adulthood and the time when he must begin to shoulder the responsibilities of being a Roman citizen.

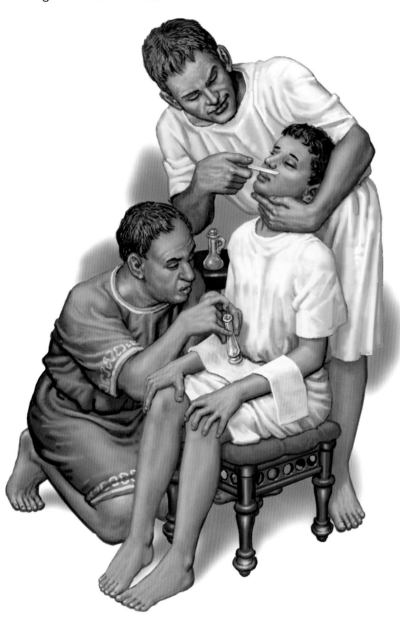

## A critical decision

A youth's future is in the hands of his father. Among the lower classes it is traditional for a son to follow in his father's trade. But among the better families, a political career is considered essential. And in Rome the law and politics are almost one and the same thing. However, nothing is easily achieved without first showing a degree of typically Roman prowess in the army.

Before starting on a political career, young men are expected to have spent at least ten years in the army, first as a military tribune or junior officer and then possibly as adjutant to a

### The senior magistrates

The two consuls are the most senior officials. They manage the affairs of the Senate and the army. After their year in office they become proconsuls (governors) in the provinces.

Eight *praetors* are elected to be judges in the law courts.

Four *aediles* are selected to look after civic affairs—the grain supply, markets, public buildings, and streets. They also organize and pay for public games.

Twenty *quaestors* look after financial matters. Although elected, they are not necessarily senators. The office is an important step on the political ladder—anyone elected as a *quaestor* automatically becomes a senator.

Every five years two *censors* are chosen from among former consuls and serve for 18 months. They revise the Senate's membership, removing undesirables and enrolling new senators.

For a Roman youth, his first shave is a religious event. Here Maximus Valerius honors his son Quintus by performing the ceremony himself. Soon, he will introduce the youth to his colleagues in the Forum and start Quintus properly on the *cursus honorum*.

The cuttings from a boy's first shave are carefully preserved in a glass phial and offered to the household's gods in thanksgiving for his having reached manhood.

At the age of 15 or 16 he may also take off his childhood *bulla* (*see page 19*), discard his *toga praetexta* and put on the *toga virilis* of an adult. Dressed thus as a man, his father leads him into the Forum amid much ceremony to introduce the young Roman to his colleagues and the senior magistrates.

gate (*see page 58*). However, there are some exceptions. When a student of rhetoric shows great aptitude as a legal apprentice, he might find himself put on the first steps of the *cursus honorum* without having done any military service.

## The *cursus honorum*

It means "course of honors" and describes the traditional career path of a senator. There are five political offices on the *cursus honorum* a candidate may aspire to, each tougher to achieve than the last. They are quaestor, then aedile, praetor, consul, and finally censor—few men ever reach this distinguished office.

But in the imperial period, there are several more intermediate steps, the first of which is a place on the board of 20 minor magistrates known as the *vigintivirate*. Among this board's duties lies the responsibility for keeping Rome's streets in a clean state—no easy task.

## The imperial civil service

Men of the equestrian order make up the bulk of Rome's middle class. Unlike senators, equestrians may engage in business or, at a lower social level, even trade. But for many, the imperial civil service offers a fine career. In earlier, simpler Republican times administrative offices were held on an annual basis by a senatorial magistrate. In the imperial era most magistracies are honorary and the real work is done by equestrian bureaucrats.

For instance, the functions of the *aediles* are really handled by officials such as the *praefectus annonae*—an equestrian in charge of the grain supply. There are also various *curatores* (boards) to look after the roads (*curatores viarum*), the water supply and aqueducts (*curatores aquarum*), and public buildings (*curatores operum publicorum*).

The ultimate prize is to

Grain silos on the banks of the Nile: Egypt's governor—the *praefectus Aegypti*—has one of the most responsible jobs in the Empire, for it is from here that most of Rome's bread grain comes. Any disruption to the supply quickly leads to famine in the city—and riots soon follow.

The more important the magistrate, the more lictors he has in attendance. Consuls have 12 lictors each, and *praetors* when outside Italy have six lictors each. The emperor is preceded by 24 lictors. They carry a *fasces* as a symbol of authority.

govern a province. This function only goes to a senator who has been either a praetor or a consul. However, the post of his assistant in charge of finances, the *procurator*, is filled by an equestrian. This office provides plenty of opportunities for financial gain and often real power whenever the governor is absent or has been recalled.

The two highest equestrian offices are those of *praefectus praetorio* (Praetorian Prefect) and *praefectus Aegypti* (Prefect of Egypt). The first is one of two commanders of the Praetorian Guard, the soldiers who protect the emperor and the imperial family. The second is appointed by the emperor to govern "Rome's granary"—Egypt. Both posts are therefore only given to dependable men—and the emperor rarely trusts any senators since most want to curb his powers whenever they can.

### Minor bureaucrats

*Apparitores* are public servants, such as scribes, who attend magistrates. They receive a salary from the state, and are generally freedmen or the sons of freedmen.

*Lictores* attend magistrates, walking in front in single file carrying the *fasces*, as a sign of the magistrate's imperium. The *fasces* are a bundle of rods. Originally they surrounded an ax as a symbol of the king's right to whip and execute people, but now only the emperor's lictors carry the ax as well.

# A Senator's Day

Dawn's light cuts through the shadows cast by the city's seven hills. Daylight hours are precious, so even before the sun has risen above the roofs, Maximus Valerius, a busy senator, begins his day.

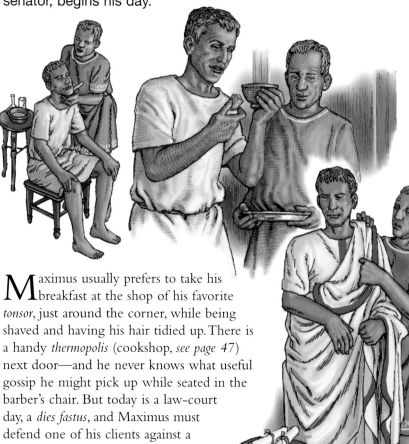

**M**aximus usually prefers to take his breakfast at the shop of his favorite *tonsor*, just around the corner, while being shaved and having his hair tidied up. There is a handy *thermopolis* (cookshop, *see page 47*) next door—and he never knows what useful gossip he might pick up while seated in the barber's chair. But today is a law-court day, a *dies fastus*, and Maximus must defend one of his clients against a charge of theft. So he contents himself with being barbered at home by his body slave, Eumolpus.

Then there is barely time to swallow some bread dipped in watered wine before he must don his senatorial toga, amid much fussing over by Eumolpus, to be ready for his clients. They are waiting for him in the *atrium*.

The clients of Maximus arrive. It is the daily duty of a client to go to his patron's home in the morning and be in attendance, even if there is no specific purpose to his visit.

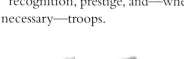

## The patronage system

Roman society is centered on patronage. People without the legal protection of a family—newcomers to Rome, for instance, freed slaves, or perhaps a young man who has had to leave his family—can attach themselves to the *paterfamilias* of an existing family. They are known as *clientes* (clients), and their protectors as *patroni* (patrons). The *cliens* gives his *patronus* social and political support in return for financial and legal protection.

A patron's social stature is judged by the number of his clients. In turn, he may himself be a client to a more powerful patron, in a chain reaching up to the emperor, the ultimate patron.

The patronage system is vital in order to make headway in Roman business—particularly for senators. They are prohibited from engaging in trade, so to supplement income derived from their country estates, they use their clients to run businesses for them in their name.

In its most complex form, patronage extends to whole cities or even nations. A family might act as patron to a provincial city, advising it on administrative matters and lobbying on its behalf in the Senate. In return, the client-city provides the family with financial gifts, recognition, prestige, and—when necessary—troops.

## Forum business and gossip

Maximus listens to his clients' petitions. One needs only a new cloak, another requires a substantial loan to further a business deal. Some are angling for a dinner invitation tonight. In turn, Maximus tells them what he wants them to do for him.

Then there is just time to check in on his youngest son (who is fretting over some composition problem with his tutor) before setting out for the Forum. His retinue of clients accompanies him, and soon they are mingling with other senators and their clients, exchanging views on the various political matters before the Senate.

Leaving the clients either to go about their daily business or to lounge around in the Forum, Maximus enters the Curia (Senate House), *top right*, to hear a debate on the merits of a new law the emperor has proposed. There is little doubt about the outcome—what the emperor wants the emperor usually gets.

A daily visit to the Forum gives senators like Maximus the opportunity to exchange current political gossip with their fellow senators and glance at the *Daily Gazette*, which is posted in a prominent position.

## In the basilica

Maximus cannot stay to the end of the discussion because it is time to walk across the Forum—clients back in attendance—to the Basilica Julia, where the law court is sitting today to hear cases of petty theft (*see pages 72–73 on Roman law*).

In defense of his client accused of stealing, his excellent rhetoric he learned as a young student in Athens sways the jury and wins the day. The presiding praetor absolves Maximus's young client of any wrongdoing.

## A bath before dinner

After a wearing morning's labor, Maximus retires to his favorite bath complex for exercise, a massage, and a cleansing bath before returning home in the mid-afternoon to prepare himself for the planned banquet.

Yesterday, he dined out at a fellow senator's *domus*, but this evening there are several guests invited, and the revelry may well go late into the night. Just as well that tomorrow is a public festival—he can stay in bed a little longer than usual.

A busy working day ends with a visit to the baths to relax as well as get clean, ready to return home for dinner.

## Shops and Shopkeepers

No civilization before has provided its citizens with so many amenities. Every street is lined with small shops offering all kinds of goods and services.

The width of city streets varies enormously, from wide thoroughfares to the narrowest alleyways negotiable only on foot. In the more prosperous areas, the streets are paved with stone and edged with *crepidines*, raised walkways that protect pedestrians from dirt during the day and the constant stream of wheeled traffic at night (*see "Sleepless in Rome"*). At intervals, stepping stones enable pedestrians to cross from one side to the other without descending into the dusty roadway.

A typically busy street corner in Rome. At the left, a man eats his free load of bread, ignoring the street seller behind. A beggar lies beside a public fountain, tortured by the smells of hot food coming from the *thermopolium* next to him. On the other side of the street, a *caupona* does a roaring trade with thirsty customers.

**Below:** A carved relief depicts a shopkeeper showing customers his wares in a fabric store, with lengths of cloth and cushions hanging from an overhead rail.

## Tabernae

Regardless of its size, every street is lined with workshops or small store units. Few shopkeepers or craftsmen own the premises where they work, since almost all property in Rome and the major provincial cities is in the ownership of the senatorial and wealthier equestrian families.

Shops are usually a single room at the front of a private *domus*, or several in a row under an *insula*. These are called *tabernae*. Larger *tabernae* have a second room behind for storage. Many shops have a solid masonry counter for the display of goods, and in the case of a *caupona* (tavern), large ceramic jars are built into the counter's surface, which are used for serving wine and foodstuffs. You can be certain that every city block has several such taverns.

As in Greece, intersections of streets have a religious significance and there will always be a shrine to some ancient guardian deity on the corner. Intersections are also a popular site for a *caupona*. It is said that when a Roman gives a stranger directions, you can tell what sort of person he is if he directs you either by the shrines or the signs of the taverns.

## A daily trip to the *pistor*

The city's poor (as well as any citizens who rent an apartment) have no cooking facilities at home, and must rely on others to cook for them. As numerous as *cauponae* are the *thermopolii*. These cook shops are found on every block, serving hot sausages, hot meat pies, stews, bread, cheese, figs, dates, nuts, cakes, and wine. The huge demand for these cook shops and snack bars is such that Rome has close to 10,000 of them.

Grain prices are subsidized by the state for the poor, and some is even given away free to the very poorest people on a monthly basis. Bread is the Roman's staple diet, and every day people take their wheat to the local baker, or *pistor*, who bakes their loaves for them.

## An unpleasant trade

For passersby and those unlucky enough to live close to one, a dyer and fuller's workshop is the least popular on the block. The stench is often terrible, especially in the heat of summer. Fulling is a form of dry-cleaning process in which cloth is trod in a tub containing a solution of decayed urine. This is collected regularly from the public latrines (the emperor Vespasian taxed it). With so many togas needing frequent cleaning, fullers are busy tradespeople.

In its raw form, the purple dye so loved by Romans also has an unpleasant smell, since it is derived from shellfish. The rotting piles of discarded fish parts add to the unpleasant odor.

### Sleepless in Rome

The noise and clamor in Rome is terrible. The cries of vendors selling sausages and pease pudding mingle with the shouts of peddlers and street entertainers, the hammering of metalworkers, and drunken soldiers on leave. Even at night there is no peace, for wagons—forbidden by Julius Caesar to enter Rome during the day because of the appalling congestion—rattle constantly along the streets in every hour of darkness. Only those who can afford a country villa ever escape the noise on the few occasions they can get away.

# The Major Crafts

With a mania for organization, Roman businesses are efficiently run at every level. Many tradesmen—such as armorers, brick-makers, and bakers—are so important to the economy that they run under a form of state control.

Romans make no distinction between a craft and industry, and across the Roman world workshops range from small, localized businesses to large-scale mass production centers whose wares travel the empire. The commonest craft is the potter's.

## Pottery

The main pottery-making centers are based in Gaul and northern Italy. Some coarse pottery for local use is handmade, but most is wheel-made. Very fine pots such as *terra sigillata* (Samian ware) are made in molds. Immense quantities of Samian ware are made and exported to every corner of the empire. *Terra sigillata* is usually a glossy red, made from a clay so fine that it needs no glaze to give the finished pot a shiny surface. Pots usually have raised decorations of fine detail, thanks to the mold system.

The red color is obtained by firing in the oxygen-rich atmosphere of a kiln. By closing the kiln's vents toward the end of the firing process, the reducing (oxygen-starved) atmosphere turns the pot a deep black, similar to the process used by the Greeks in black- and red-figure ware.

Some potteries specialize in making thin-walled vessels as drinking beakers, others in mortars used for food preparation. These are large and made strong by incorporating grit into the clay.

But the biggest sector of the industry is involved in making building materials and amphorae, the universal means of transporting liquids and free-flowing commodities such as grain (*see also page 65*).

Milling grain to make flour and baking bread are often done on the same premises. The miller uses donkeys to turn his rotary mill to grind the wheat.

## Woodworking

Wood is used extensively in the construction of furniture and carvings, buildings, ships, wagons, tools, barrels, and fortifications. The Roman carpenter attains a high standard of workmanship with his range of excellent hand tools. Axes, adzes, chisels, files, and saw blades are made from iron, and allow for very fine work.

Planes are used for smoothing wood. Some have the iron blade set in a wooden body, while more expensive ones are all of iron. Planes with an iron sole are more hard-wearing and accurate.

Lathes are used for turning wood to make bowls, chair and table legs, and small table tops. Holes are made with a bow-drill, and pieces of wood are joined with mortise-and-tenon or dovetail joints. Iron nails, wooden pegs, and animal skin glue are also used to join pieces, but the Romans do not have screws.

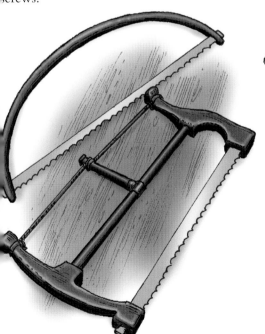

**Far left:** Carving of a butcher's shop. **Left:** A farmer uses oxen to pull a cart laden with meat for the market. The guilds (*collegia*) of meat wholesalers have their own markets. Guilds dealing in foodstuffs are usually under state control, since their goods are vital to the wellbeing of citizens.

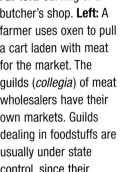

**1**

**2**

**Left:** The bow saw has a blade fixed to the ends of a piece of wood bent into a semicircle. The stress in the wood keeps the blade taut. In the H-frame saw, the blade is fixed across the bottom of the H, while a cord across the top keeps the saw blade taut.

## Lamps

Roman houses are lit at night by means of oil lamps, made from bronze or more commonly clay. A lamp consists of a chamber for the oil (preferably olive oil), a hole for filling, a short spout to hold the linen wick, and sometimes a handle. Lamps are manufactured almost everywhere.

## Glass

The invention of glassblowing in the 1st century BCE has raised the making of glass to a high art form. The glassblower dips a long iron tube into molten glass and then blows down the tube to form a bubble. By reheating, the bubble can be shaped by many means—spinning, twirling, rolling it along a flat surface—to any desired shape.

Before glassblowing, glassware was too expensive for any except the rich, but now it is a low-cost item, and many households boast a range of drinking, serving, and decorative glass utensils. Expensive pieces produced for wealthy owners have decoration formed by cutting shapes (facets) or by grinding the surface into rough-and-shiny images.

**3**

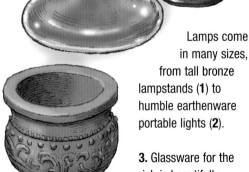

Lamps come in many sizes, from tall bronze lampstands (**1**) to humble earthenware portable lights (**2**).

**3.** Glassware for the rich is beautifully crafted.

**4**

**4.** An earthenware cup.

## Metalworking

Gold and silversmiths' workshops turn out jewelry including necklaces, earrings, bracelets, and pendants. Most objects are made from sheet metal formed by hammering the ingot on an anvil, although strand wire is used in chains and earrings. Silver is also used to make plates, decorated by engraving, chasing, and gilding.

Copper is most commonly used as an alloy with tin to produce bronze or with zinc to produce brass. Bronze is used for tableware, coins, armor and some weapons.

Large hollow statues are made by casting bronze using the "lost-wax" method. A roughly shaped clay core is made with a beeswax model around it. This is covered by clay and bronze pins are inserted to keep the inner core in place when the wax is melted in the firing. Molten bronze is poured into the gap left by the wax. The outer clay mold is carefully removed in pieces so it may be reused, and the inner core taken out through the base of the finished figure. The hole is sealed over with bronze, or covered by a

pedestal. This enables the mass production of objects such as portraits of the emperor.

Lead is used to produce weights, but most importantly, sheets of lead are used in plumbing—for lining water tanks, making guttering, water pipes, and bath linings.

## Leather

Leather is important because it's used in a range of articles—shoes, saddles, harnesses, bags, tents, buckets, jugs, some clothing, door hinges, and military shields. Leather is processed at tanneries—those working under contract to the army are huge.

After being treated to prevent bacterial decay—by salting or sun-drying—animal hides are washed and then soaked in a lime solution to make them more receptive to the tanning liquids. The lime also loosens any hair or wool, which has to be scraped off by hand. The hide is then tanned in a solution of wood bark before being sent to a leather-maker for finishing, coloring, and cutting.

## Guilds and trade associations

Most trades are regulated by a guild or trade association known as a *collegium* (*collegia* in the plural). A *collegium* sets out standards that its members must maintain and in some cases even dictates minimum and maximum prices. It also deals with industrial issues like negotiating state contracts, running political campaigns, lobbying the government, providing legal aid for its members, and social activities for their families.

Almost every aspect of Roman commerce is covered by a *collegium*. For instance, the *collegium pistorum* looks after millers and bakers, while butchers have three *collegia*— *suariorum* (pork), *boarii* (beef), and *pecuarii* (mutton). Even river boatmen, or *nautae*, who operate barges along the empire's rivers, have their own *collegium*.

Not all associations are commercial in nature. The most august is the *collegium pontificum*, or college of priests. Many poorer Romans belong to funeral societies, called *collegia funeraticia*, to ensure a proper burial. In return for regular payments, the *collegium* covers the cost of funerals for its members. It also guarantees a place in a *columbarium*, a mass tomb where ashes in urns are placed in small niches, usually marked by memorial

A knife-maker and merchant named Cornelius Atimetus (standing on the right) shows a customer samples of his cutlery.

laques and portrait sculptures. The tomb resembles a dovecote, hence its name—*olumba* is Latin for "dove."

Although trade associations have many enefits for their members, there is a disadvantage, especially in industries vital to he security of the empire. It is very easy for he emperor to regulate a *collegium*'s activities and make a voluntary association into a compulsory one. This is particularly true for he mining and building trades (especially hose involved in fortifications), and that of rms manufacturers and armorers. In many ases, compulsion extends to enforcing that son follows his father in trade.

## Quarrying and mining

ince the beginning of the imperial era, Rome has stepped up the quarrying of good tone enormously. Quarries producing the inest travertine and marble are under mperial control. Their output is used for acing public buildings, columns, and culptures. Nearly all of the major quarries re near rivers or the sea for ease of transport.

Stone blocks are cut from their beds by driving iron wedges. The blocks are roughly dressed at the quarry face using picks and dzes. A massive, multi-bladed saw may be used where a strong water flow is available to power the machine. This is particularly useful or cutting thin slices of travertine used in acing brick buildings.

With the exception of agriculture, mining is the largest industry of the Roman Empire. Gold, silver, copper, tin, lead, and iron are the major metals mined. In both quarries and mines, slaves provide the labor, but in the mines the slaves have a terrible and often very short life.

In most cases, the raw ore is smelted or refined at the mines and then formed into ingots for transportation to manufacturing centers to be made into artifacts. Metals are used for the production of coinage, to make arms and armor, and many household utensils and luxury goods.

A pharmacy offers the public all kinds of medicinal potions, as well as ladies' cosmetics. The pharmaceutical trade employs women as well as men. Found on many streets, they provide health care to people— something that slaves working in appalling conditions in the quarries can never hope for. Their lives are miserable and short.

# Builders and Building

Augustus boasted that he found Rome built of brick and left her clothed in marble. However, with a few grand exceptions, most buildings are of concrete, brick, and timber.

The development of concrete in the late 3rd century BCE has allowed Roman architects to design stronger, taller, and much larger buildings than ever before. Concrete, known as *opus caementicium*, is made with an aggregate of stone, brick, or tile set in mortar made with lime, water, and a volcanic sand called *pozzolana*, which gives extra strength and is even hydraulic (hardens under water).

Foundations are laid by digging a trench and raising layers of wooden shuttering, filling in each course with concrete until the desired height is reached. This might be as much as 16–20 feet for a large temple.

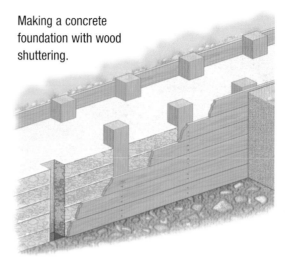

Making a concrete foundation with wood shuttering.

**Right:** Men belonging to the *collegia fabrorum* (the builders' guild) are constructing a barrel vault, one of several forming a new basilica.

## Raising walls

Concrete walls are constructed with stone or brick facings, and known by their style. There are three main styles, as shown in the illustrations.

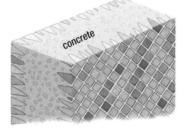

**Right:** *Opus reticularum* is a facing made of pyramid-shaped stones or fired bricks, making an attractive diagonal diamond pattern.

**Left:** *Opus incertum* is a facing made of small, roughly shaped stones.

**Right:** *Opus testaceum* is a facing made of fired bricks cut into triangles; rectangular bricks are also used. An outer facing of thin travertine or marble panels covers many public buildings.

travertine

While the lower floor of an *insula* is usually built with one form or other of faced concrete wall, the upper floors have walls constructed from a timber frame filled in with rubble and mortar. It is a cheap method, but a terrible fire hazard.

This form of wall called *opus craticum* is liable to catch fire and collapse unexpectedly.

Roofing tiles

*tegula*

*imbric*

back

front

## Roofing

Roofs are made of wooden frames covered with flat tiles made of terracotta, a clay strengthened with coarse sand. The main rectangular tile is called a *tegula*; the half-round tile that covers the gaps between *tegulae* is called an *imbric*. *Imbric*es are also used as ridge tiles where the two slopes of a roof meet.

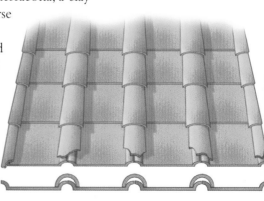

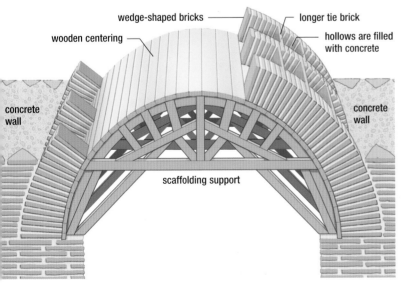

wedge-shaped bricks

wooden centering

longer tie brick

hollows are filled with concrete

concrete wall

concrete wall

scaffolding support

## Arches and barrel vaults

Concrete makes it possible to build larger arches than ever before. The most common form is called a brick barrel vault. The arch is formed from wedge-shaped bricks arranged in several rows. At intervals, a longer brick ties the individual arch rows together. The spaces in between are filled with concrete.

Precise carpentry is required during construction. The centering or formwork is supported by scaffolding, over which the bricks are placed and mortared together. Once the concrete has cured (set solid), the centering can be removed and the inside of the arch may be faced with plaster, travertine, or marble.

# Farming

Most farming land is owned by aristocratic Romans. Despising trade, business, and manufacture, it is beneath a Roman man's dignity to be anything except a warrior, a magistrate, or a farmer—with slaves to do all the work.

During the Punic Wars with Carthage, many owners of small farms had to leave their land to join the army. The farms fell into neglect and many were devastated by Hannibal's Carthaginian army. When the wars ended in Rome's victory, the small farmers could not afford to repair the damage and their land was bought up by rich landowners, who soon turned much of Italy into giant farm estates called *latifundia*.

Despite several attempts since to return land to small farmers (*see "The alimenta of Nerva"*), the *latifundia* still dominate Italy and many other parts of the empire.

**1.** A wooden-framed plow with an iron blade is used for turning over the fields ready for planting. Because of Italy's mild winters, seed is sown in the fall, and may be again in the spring.

**2.** Olive oil stored in jars buried in the ground is used for a form of soap, in cooking, and as fuel for lamps.

**3.** Most farms have a small vineyard for growing grapes, and a grape press.

**4.** The estate overseer has a modest but comfortably appointed house, where the owner stays overnight on a visit. However, the owner is more likely to remain at his nearby villa (*see page 38*).

**5.** The threshing floor, where horses are driven over grain to separate the wheat from the stalks and chaff.

**6.** The "winnowed" grain is then milled to make flour for bread.

**7.** Romans have brought many useful inventions to farming, such as the harvesting machine.

**8.** Pigeons are a popular dish, so most farms have a dovecote and keep pigeons for food in the winter.

**0.** Horses are not bred or farming, but for the rmy, which pays well.

**11.** Cattle are kept more for plowing than for their milk or meat. Romans prefer the milk of water buffalo, which is used to make cheese.

**12.** Market gardening is a profitable source of a senator's income. Many kinds of vegetables and fruit including cabbages, lettuces, radishes, carrots, leeks, beans, onions, figs, pears, and apples are grown on the plots.

**13.** Chickens, ducks, and geese are kept in large numbers for their eggs and meat.

**14.** Sheep are kept for their milk and meat, but especially for their wool, used in making togas.

**15.** Goats provide milk, and their hair is used for making rope and sacking.

**9.** The farm has several beehives to provide honey, the only sweetener Romans have for their food.

Hundreds of slaves are used for every task. Privileged slaves have simple quarters attached to the main farm buildings, but most field laborers have to make do with sharing the cattle sheds, stables, or just a ditch.

## An imperial farm

Agriculture is the primary industry of the Roman Empire, and the typical imperial farm produces a variety of goods. Cereals are grown, but not to a great extent, since large areas of arable land are scarce in Italy. Grain is imported in vast quantities from Egypt, North Africa, and Sicily. Local grain is mostly grown to provide the livestock with feed through the winter. The main commodities are cattle, oil, wine, and vegetables.

Given the perishable nature of most produce, farms are usually dedicated to growing food for the inhabitants of nearby towns. Those sited close to a major road leading to Rome can make a lot of money from selling luxury items, rapidly transported in the cool of the night to the city, when carts are allowed inside the walls.

Although he only ruled for a short time, Nerva was one of Rome's best emperors.

### The *alimenta* of Nerva

Thanks to Emperor Nerva (96–98 CE), small farmers now receive state aid through a program called the *alimenta*. Under this plan, small farmers pledge their land as security and are allowed to borrow up to a 12th of its value from the state treasury, at a rate of 5 percent interest on the loan. However, this interest is not paid to the treasury but to the farmer's local township. The town then uses the money to support the children of poor parents.

The *alimenta* has been a great success. It has helped to rid Italy of poverty to some extent and also caused an upsurge in farming. Wealthy nobles now follow the emperor's example and form similar plans of their own. As a result, several thousand children are being provided for in Italy, and more in the provinces as the concept spreads.

# A Life Under Arms

No one before has taken the profession of soldiering more seriously than the Romans. From the dry shores of the southern Nile to the rain-soaked moors of northern England, legionaries keep the *pax Romana*, the Roman peace.

Aristocratic sons and those of rich fathers look to military service as an important first step in their future political careers, and their life in the army is very different from that of the ordinary soldier. A legionary signs on for a minimum of 25 years, which often becomes a much longer term.

Despite this major commitment, the army is not short of volunteers. Men join for the pay, the thrill of battle, and the chance to travel and see the world (although most of this will happen by marching for hundreds of miles). If he does well, a simple farmboy might rise through the ranks to become a centurion with 80 men under his command. He will not, however, become an officer—those ranks are only for the aristocracy.

## The new recruit

A potential recruit needs a recommendation from someone connected with the army. An accepted recruit is given funds to cover traveling expenses to his legion—which might be anywhere in the empire.

At the camp, he takes the military oath to serve the emperor, which the whole legion renews every New Year. He is then posted to a century and starts the unrelenting training that will be a daily feature of his life from this point on.

## Training

A centurion wielding a vine staff, the symbol of his rank **(1)**, puts recruits through their paces on the parade ground. Centurions—promoted for their experience and fearlessness in battle—are always loud and frightening, but those in charge of training are worse. A new recruit can do nothing right, and often feels the lash of the vine staff.

Recruits use double-weight shields and practice swords to strengthen their bodies **(2)**, attacking 6-foot high wooden stakes with their shield boss and sword. The recruit is taught to thrust with his short sword and never to use a slashing motion, which would cause harm to the man standing next to him in a real battle. He also learns to throw an overweight *pilum* javelin at a target **(3)**.

Three times a month there are route marches of 18 miles at a forced pace of 5 miles per hour, carrying the full complement of equipment (*see page 58*). Also wearing full kit, the recruit is required to run, jump, and vault over wooden horses **(4)**. He is taught how to build a defensive camp for the night. He is given training in stone-slinging, swimming, and riding, learning how to mount and dismount **(5)** fully armed from either side—without the aid of stirrups (*see "Fact box"*).

## The legionary's kit

The Roman legionary has to pay for his uniforms and its cost is taken out of his wages. Throughout his military career, all new garments and armor will have to be paid for, as well as his food.

**Above:** Recruits with skills in carpentry and engineering may be posted to a legion's sapper unit, responsible for building roads and bridges. Here, they build a trestle bridge across a river, driving piles into the river bed.

3

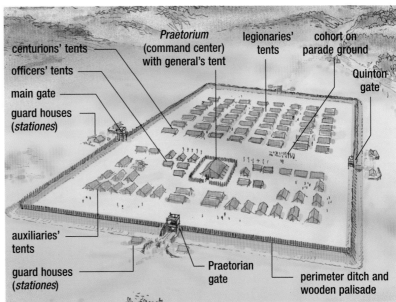

centurions' tents

officers' tents

main gate

guard houses (*stationes*)

*Praetorium* (command center) with general's tent

legionaries' tents

cohort on parade ground

Quinton gate

auxiliaries' tents

guard houses (*stationes*)

Praetorian gate

perimeter ditch and wooden palisade

**1**

**2**

**4**

**5**

**Above:** When the Roman army is marching through enemy territory, it sets up a camp every night, which is dismantled in the following morning before marching on. The process is highly organized, and every soldier knows his part. Each soldier carries two *pale*, wooden stakes. When all the soldier's stakes are put together they form the defensive palisade. Camps are always laid out in the same way, based on a square with two intersecting streets running at right angles to each other between the four gates. Each century has its own allocated space, and colored marker pegs are placed so that each cohort knows exactly where to pitch its tents.

Legionaries are flogged if they misbehave, but for mutiny the punishment is *decimatio*, when every tenth soldier is executed and from which the word "decimation" is derived.

## Fact box

Stirrups were unknown at this time. They were first introduced from southern Russia by the barbarian hordes toward the end of the 4th century CE and adopted by the Roman cavalry. By that time the Roman army was largely composed of barbarians anyway.

## Food and retirement

Since most soldiers are from the poorer classes and meat is rare in their diet, they cope well with the basic campaign diet. This is usually only hard biscuits and a porridge of cereal or chickpeas, supplemented by bacon, cheese, and a sour wine called *posca*. Preserved foods are easier to carry. A jerky of dried game or beef can stand in when salted pork is unavailable.

When a legionary reaches his full term, he may be discharged with the option of taking a sum of money or a land grant, originally Italian farmland. Now discharged veterans usually settle in the place where they have served and live in *colonia* (colonies).

**Below:** Reconstruction of Timgad in North Africa (now in Algeria), the colony for African veterans. Like a military camp, it has two main roads between the gates. Instead of the general's *Praetorium* there is the forum. The town has all the luxuries of civilized life: a theater, library, an arena (outside the picture), temples, and many public baths.

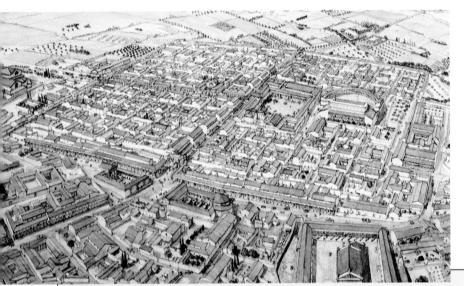

## Organization of the 28 legions

Each legion numbers about 5,000 soldiers, divided into 10 'cohorts.' A cohort is organized into six 'centuries' of about 80 men, under the command of a centurion. The centurion's second in command is called an *optio*. The legion also has several standard bearers. The most senior, the *aquilifer*, carries the legion's eagle standard, while each century has a *signifer*, who also acts as the century's banker.

Above the centuriate there are six tribunes, drawn from the wealthy equestrian class. These are temporary postings, held as a step on their political careers. Although senior to any centurion, the sensible young tribune pays attention to his centurions' experience.

Above the tribunes the *legatus* (legate) is usually a senator appointed to command a legion by the emperor. He is supported by the *praefectus castrorum* (camp prefect), an older man who has been promoted to officer class from the rank of leading centurion (*primus pilus*). The legate has a considerable staff of professionals under his command, including guard commanders, intelligence officers, torturers and executioners, veterinary surgeons, doctors, clerks and engineers, and 120 horsemen to act as scouts and dispatch riders.

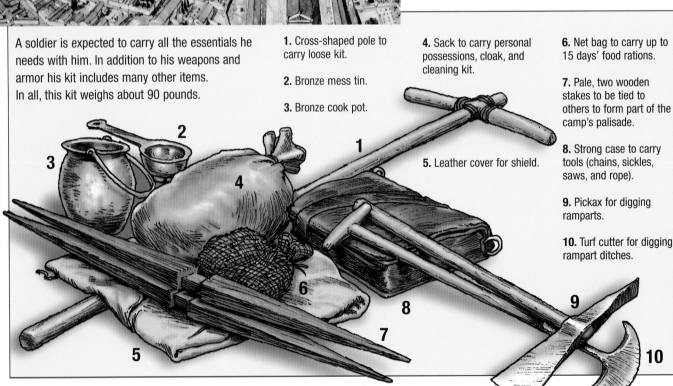

A soldier is expected to carry all the essentials he needs with him. In addition to his weapons and armor his kit includes many other items. In all, this kit weighs about 90 pounds.

**1.** Cross-shaped pole to carry loose kit.

**2.** Bronze mess tin.

**3.** Bronze cook pot.

**4.** Sack to carry personal possessions, cloak, and cleaning kit.

**5.** Leather cover for shield.

**6.** Net bag to carry up to 15 days' food rations.

**7.** Pale, two wooden stakes to be tied to others to form part of the camp's palisade.

**8.** Strong case to carry tools (chains, sickles, saws, and rope).

**9.** Pickax for digging ramparts.

**10.** Turf cutter for digging rampart ditches.

A centurion's armor is silvered. He wears leg protectors, or greaves, and has a semi-circular crest on his helmet. He wears his sword on the opposite side to the legionary.

**1.** Red-dyed tunic of wool or linen. A woolen cloak for cold weather and sleeping in.

**2.** Strong, well-ventilated *caligae* (half-boots) are laced by leather loops across the foot and up the ankle. The hob-nailed soles withstand hundreds of miles of marching. On the other hand, they can slip on hard, shiny paving.

**3.** Articulated body armor (*lorica segmenta*) is made of several metal plates attached to each other by brass hooks, hinges, and leather straps.

**4.** Metal helmet to protect the skull, ears, and back of the neck. Its projecting brow is effective in head-butting.

**5.** Leather belt to hold a sword scabbard and a groin guard of leather strips with rivetted metal disks.

**6.** Curved, rectangular shield—about 4ft by just over 2ft—made from plywood covered in leather. A metal boss protects the handhold and adds battering power. The shield's bronze rim is used for thrusting up under an opponent's chin or slashing down on an unguarded shin or foot.

**7.** Short stabbing sword (*gladius*) made of hardened iron. Its sharp sides are parallel, rapidly tapering to a wicked point. The scabbard is made of wood and leather, held together with bronze straps.

**8.** Each soldier carries two *pila*. These javelins have a wooden shaft joined to the long spearhead by a section of soft iron. This is designed to bend on impact with the ground so that the enemy cannot throw the *pilum* back.

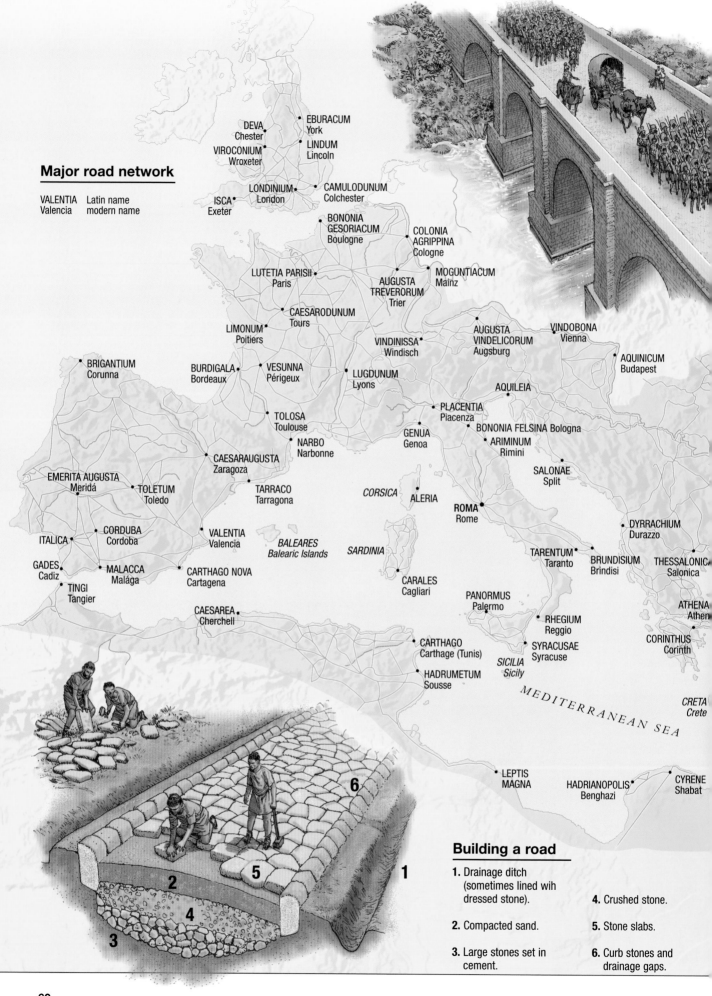

## Major road network

VALENTIA Latin name
Valencia modern name

DEVA
Chester

EBURACUM
York

LINDUM
Lincoln

VIROCONIUM
Wroxeter

ISCA
Exeter

LONDINIUM
London

CAMULODUNUM
Colchester

BONONIA
GESORIACUM
Boulogne

COLONIA
AGRIPPINA
Cologne

LUTETIA PARISII
Paris

AUGUSTA
TREVERORUM
Trier

MOGUNTIACUM
Mainz

CAESARODUNUM
Tours

LIMONUM
Poitiers

VINDINISSA
Windisch

AUGUSTA
VINDELICORUM
Augsburg

VINDOBONA
Vienna

BRIGANTIUM
Corunna

BURDIGALA
Bordeaux

VESUNNA
Périgeux

LUGDUNUM
Lyons

AQUINICUM
Budapest

AQUILEIA

PLACENTIA
Piacenza

TOLOSA
Toulouse

GENUA
Genoa

BONONIA FELSINA Bologna

ARIMINUM
Rimini

NARBO
Narbonne

CAESARAUGUSTA
Zaragoza

SALONAE
Split

EMERITA AUGUSTA
Meridá

TOLETUM
Toledo

TARRACO
Tarragona

CORSICA

ALERIA

ROMA
Rome

DYRRACHIUM
Durazzo

ITALICA

CORDUBA
Cordoba

VALENTIA
Valencia

BALEARES
Balearic Islands

SARDINIA

TARENTUM
Taranto

BRUNDISIUM
Brindisi

THESSALONIC
Salonica

GADES
Cadiz

MALACCA
Malága

CARTHAGO NOVA
Cartagena

CARALES
Cagliari

ATHENA
Athen

TINGI
Tangier

PANORMUS
Palermo

RHEGIUM
Reggio

CORINTHUS
Corinth

CAESAREA
Cherchell

CARTHAGO
Carthage (Tunis)

SYRACUSAE
Syracuse

SICILIA
Sicily

HADRUMETUM
Sousse

MEDITERRANEAN SEA

CRETA
Crete

LEPTIS
MAGNA

HADRIANOPOLIS
Benghazi

CYRENE
Shabat

## Building a road

**1.** Drainage ditch (sometimes lined wih dressed stone).

**2.** Compacted sand.

**3.** Large stones set in cement.

**4.** Crushed stone.

**5.** Stone slabs.

**6.** Curb stones and drainage gaps.

# CHAPTER 3

# Economy and Roman Law

## The Amazing Roman Road Network

Rome has brought civilization to western Europe, Asia Minor, the Middle East, Egypt, and North Africa—and most of its benefits arrive by road. Along the road system comes trade and prosperity, as well as civil law and justice.

Using concrete and advanced arch technology, Roman road engineers have little trouble in spanning rivers and steep valleys with multi-arched bridges, or viaducts.

The Romans developed out of military necessity. As the Republic expanded, military surveyors marked out the quickest routes from one place to another so that the legions could march from the city to the frontier in a few hours. They were the first all-weather routes in operation. Today the network stretches over 50,000 miles and reaches every corner of the empire.

### Building a road

The most noticeable aspect of Roman roads is the directness of their routes. Surveyors quite simply build from one sighting point to the next. Building work starts by digging twin trenches 25–30 feet apart and 3–4 feet deep. The trenches provide drainage and material excavated from them forms part of the foundations or raises the road's height.

Several layers of foundation are rammed down, sometimes bound in cement, before dressed stone blocks are cemented in place. The surface is built with a raised curve called a camber to aid drainage through gaps in the stone curb (*umbro*).

At every mile, measuring from Rome, stand milestones. These small markers give the distance and name of the nearest towns and indicate their directions, as well as commemorating the emperor of the day.

Back down the roads toward Rome come many goods, such as wild animals from Africa, silks and spices from China, glass from Sidon, and tin and wool from England. In this way roads help unite the different parts of the empire, as well as helping to keep the provinces under control.

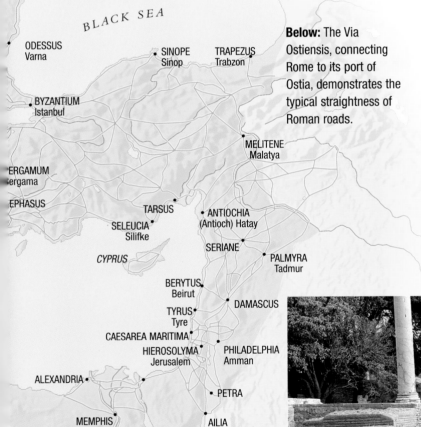

BLACK SEA

ODESSUS
Varna

SINOPE
Sinop

TRAPEZUS
Trabzon

BYZANTIUM
Istanbul

**Below:** The Via Ostiensis, connecting Rome to its port of Ostia, demonstrates the typical straightness of Roman roads.

MELITENE
Malatya

ERGAMUM
ergama

EPHASUS

TARSUS

ANTIOCHIA
(Antioch) Hatay

SELEUCIA
Silifke

SERIANE

CYPRUS

PALMYRA
Tadmur

BERYTUS
Beirut

DAMASCUS

TYRUS
Tyre

CAESAREA MARITIMA

HIEROSOLYMA
Jerusalem

PHILADELPHIA
Amman

ALEXANDRIA

PETRA

MEMPHIS

AILIA
Eilat

THEBAE
(Thebes) Luxor

# Along a Roman Road

This illustration combines many of the features a traveler encounters when journeying from one town to another.

Most Roman vehicles are built to a standard gauge (the width along the axle between the wheels) of 5 feet. The gauge is not enforced, but the ruts in the stone paving formed by centuries of wheeled traffic make for an uncomfortable ride if only one wheel runs in a rut.

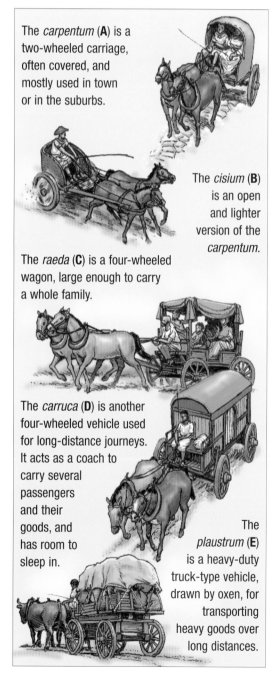

The *carpentum* (**A**) is a two-wheeled carriage, often covered, and mostly used in town or in the suburbs.

The *cisium* (**B**) is an open and lighter version of the *carpentum*.

The *raeda* (**C**) is a four-wheeled wagon, large enough to carry a whole family.

The *carruca* (**D**) is another four-wheeled vehicle used for long-distance journeys. It acts as a coach to carry several passengers and their goods, and has room to sleep in.

The *plaustrum* (**E**) is a heavy-duty truck-type vehicle, drawn by oxen, for transporting heavy goods over long distances.

**1.** State-controlled guesthouses called *mansiones* are built at intervals of about 15 Roman miles in civilized regions. Even though some are quite large, they are not very comfortable. However, *mansiones* are often better than local inns.

**2.** Enterprising people operate small food and drink shops (*tabernae*) and sometimes offer accommodation to guests. Unfortunately, many inns are dirty, the food terrible, and their owners little more than bandits. Inns tend to attract local craftsmen to set up workshops and take advantage of the passing trade to sell their goods.

**3.** Milestones are placed on the roadside. The Roman mile is about 5000 feet long, based on a thousand paces (*mille* is Latin for a thousand).

**4.** Post stations are set up along main roads between 6 and 15 Roman miles apart. They are run by the *cursus publicus*, the government postal system, which operates throughout the empire. Official messengers on state business can change horses at a post station, or hand their message on to a relay rider at the end of their shift.

**5.** The military has priority over everyone on the roads. Civilian traffic gets out of the way as quickly as possible to allow a century of soldiers to march past.

# Military and Merchant Shipping

Unlike their seafaring neighbors the Greeks, Romans have never liked the sea. Nevertheless, Rome boasts a vast merchant fleet to serve the empire's trade and a large navy to keep the seas safe from pirates.

When it is not engaged in open warfare, the Roman navy—which is under the control of the army—spends much of its time fighting the many pirates who threaten merchant shipping, especially in the eastern Mediterranean.

Naval ships are based on the Greek *trireme*, but the heavy battleship of the Roman fleet is called a *quinquereme*. Its name comes from the five (*quinque*) oarsmen manning each bank of three oars. The ship carries a complement of 300 oarsmen, 120 marines, and 50 crew to man the sail and steering oars. Under full manpower, a *quinquereme* can travel at about 12 miles per hour.

## Battle tactics

The Greeks tended to ram and sink enemy vessels instead of boarding them, but Romans prefer to treat a sea battle like one on land. Although the warships are equipped with armored beaks for ramming, they also have a *corvus*.

The size and weight of a *quinquereme* equipped with a *corvus* makes the ship unstable, and so for general naval campaigns the lighter, more maneuverable *trireme* is still widely used.

The frame of a merchant ship's hull is made of oak, and the planking cut from pine or elder. The ship is completely decked to form a cargo hold below, and usually has small deckhouses near the bow and toward the stern. Four sails power the ship—two top sails, the main sail, and a forward steering sail, which assists the two steering oars at the stern.

**The *corvus***
A stout pillar of wood supports a boarding bridge on a rope pulley. At the end of the bridge is a penetrating metal spike called a *corvus*, named for its resemblance to a raven's sharp beak. When the bridge is rapidly lowered, the *corvus* slams into the enemy's deck, hitching the two ships together and allowing the marines to swarm aboard the enemy ship.

The *amphora* is one of the commonest items made by potters, since they are used to transport a wide range of goods. The shape of the *amphora* allows for many to be stacked in a ship's hold, several levels deep, and held securely against the motion of a rough sea.

## The cargo ship

Unlike warships, merchantmen rely more on sail power than on oars. They are generally built to a standard pattern, but vary greatly in length and width, depending on the purpose for which they have been designed. A small vessel might measure 60 feet long by 17 wide, but larger ships can be as much as 100 feet long by 30 feet wide.

Cargo ships carry all kinds of goods over great distances, usually stored in the all-purpose clay jars called *amphorae*. With a high neck, two handles, and a pointed bottom, the *amphora* is designed for speedy and secure stacking. *Amphorae* contain every essential food item, including olives, olive oil, wine, grain, and pickled fish.

The crews of Roman navy ships row hard in this section of carved relief from the famous Column of Trajan. Galleys are crowded, cramped, and uncomfortable vessels and, like their merchant counterparts, naval crews spend their nights ashore where they can safely light cook fires and stretch out to sleep.

## Navigation

The ship's captain has no instruments to help him find his way across the open sea, but Roman merchantmen do not hug the coast as did the Greeks. They have several books to advise them of the best routes across the Mediterranean Sea and the various kinds of weather to expect at different times of the year. To calculate where he is, a captain looks at the heavenly bodies—the sun, and at night the moon, stars, and planets—to judge his position, knowing the speed and direction of the wind.

## Financing a voyage

Some captains own their own ship, but most work in the employ of rich Romans of the equestrian class. Although senators are prohibited from engaging in trade, they can use their wealth indirectly to finance fleets of ships through a client of non-senatorial rank and make a healthy profit from the proceeds of a successful round-trip.

Merchant shippers also employ agents at various ports around the empire to make sure there will be a cargo to collect for the return voyage to Rome. The agent also takes a cut of the profits. Transfers of money are made simple through the banking system (*see pages 68–69*).

## Life onboard

The crew's provisions—stored in containers such as amphorae, baskets, or sacks—are kept either below the deck or in the small forward cabin. The supply for a voyage includes liquids (water, wine, oil, and the fish sauce called *garum*), and solid foods (cereals, olives, fresh or dried fruit, dried beans and legumes, smoked or salted meats).

Personal objects belonging to the crew or to passengers are also stored in the cabin. These include clothes, shoes, rings, and playing dice to help while away the time. Coins and a lever scale are carried for commercial transactions, once dry land is reached.

Mariners are among the most superstitious of Romans, and small portable altars and images of the gods are set up onboard ship. When not manning the sails and steering oars, the crew are busy repairing sails with bone needles, or fishing to enrich the modest food supply with fresh produce.

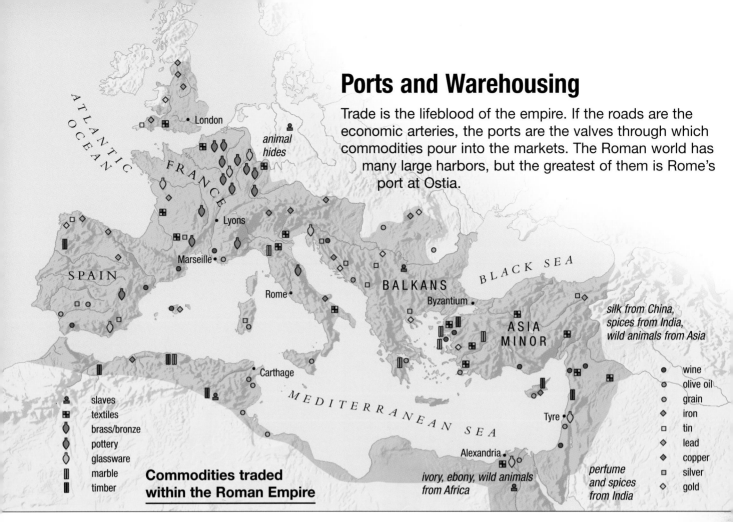

# Ports and Warehousing

Trade is the lifeblood of the empire. If the roads are the economic arteries, the ports are the valves through which commodities pour into the markets. The Roman world has many large harbors, but the greatest of them is Rome's port at Ostia.

**Commodities traded within the Roman Empire**

*animal hides*

*silk from China, spices from India, wild animals from Asia*

*ivory, ebony, wild animals from Africa*

*perfume and spices from India*

- slaves
- textiles
- brass/bronze
- pottery
- glassware
- marble
- timber

- wine
- olive oil
- grain
- iron
- tin
- lead
- copper
- silver
- gold

Map labels: ATLANTIC OCEAN, London, FRANCE, Lyons, Marseille, SPAIN, Rome, Carthage, MEDITERRANEAN SEA, BALKANS, Byzantium, BLACK SEA, ASIA MINOR, Tyre, Alexandria

Ostia lies close to the mouth of the Tiber. In the late Republic, its single, long quay was sufficient for the amount of ships calling in to unload, but in the early imperial period the enormous growth in sea-borne trade outstripped capacity. The silt carried downriver by the Tiber has also clogged up the estuary, making it hard for any but the smallest vessels to dock there.

During his 41–54 CE reign, Emperor Claudius constructed a new harbor on the coast about a mile north of Ostia. It is simply called Portus. This has led to a decline in old Ostia's commercial fortunes, but the town thrives as a pleasant retirement center and a place for Romans to have second homes away from the bustle of the city. Ostia has all the amenities necessary for comfortable living, such as shops, a forum, temples, public latrines, and plenty of baths.

Portus has since been enlarged by Trajan (97–117) with a six-sided second basin, new warehouses, and a canal linking the harbor to the Tiber beyond the silted up stretch of the river. From Portus, along the canal, and up the river, the bargemen transport goods to warehouses in Rome, ready for distribution.

Like all Roman harbors, Portus has a lighthouse for night navigation. The largest lighthouse in the Roman world is the Pharos at Alexandria. Standing over 100 feet high, this wonder of the world uses huge, polished metal plates to reflect the light of a fire.

## Temporary storage of goods

Warehouses (*horrea*) stand alongside the port's quays. Built of wood or stone with tile roofs, some of them are huge. The Horrea Galbana, which stands in Rome near to the Tiber, covers over 25,200 square yards. Many warehouses consist of rows of secure rooms around a central courtyard, although pressure of space often means the courtyard gets filled in with more rooms.

Warehouses are used for storing goods from all over the empire, from building materials to foodstuffs, especially grain from Egypt and North Africa. Grain warehouses have raised timber floors to keep out vermin and to allow a good circulation of air beneath to control the temperature and humidity.

## Customs duty

Goods being imported or exported are subject to a *portorium*, a customs tax. The tax is levied at all frontiers, but the great ports are the busiest places for customs officers, and there may be as many as a hundred functionaries checking ships' cargo manifests. The tax, which goes straight to the emperor's treasury, or the *fiscus*, is usually levied at a rate of 2 to 2.5 percent of the goods' value. But some luxury commodities attract much higher rates, sometimes as much as 25 percent.

**Above:** Rome's harbor, Portus at Ostia, was built by Emperor Claudius (the left basin) and enlarged by Trajan with a six-sided basin. A canal links the port to the Tiber (at extreme top right) and Rome.

**Below:** At Ostia, goods from seagoing ships are transferred to barges that are then towed up the Tiber to Rome's busy docks by teams of oxen. There, vast tracts of warehouses await the imported wares.

# Money, Banking, and Treasuries

As in all other matters Roman, coins, weights, and measures are strictly controlled, with special government departments to look after them.

The Romans adopted coins relatively late, in about the middle of the 3rd century BCE, accepting the system from the Greek cities of southern Italy. Early Roman coins did not carry portraits on the obverse (front). The first to do so was struck in 197 BCE to commemorate the victory of Titus Quinctius Flaminus over the Macedonians. Portraits on coins disappeared again until the time of Julius Caesar, some 150 years later. Now, all coins carry a portrait of the emperor on the obverse.

Roman coins are derived from a standard-weight bar of bronze known as an *as* (plural *asses*). The initial *as* weighed a Roman pound (just under 11.5 ounces), but was later reduced in weight until by 217 BCE an *as* weighed only 9.5 ounces.

The highest denomination coin of the empire is the gold *aureus*. However, the coin most commonly used is the silver *denarius*. Both are minted under the emperor's direct control. Only bronze and copper coins, which are less valuable, may be produced by provincial mints. The most widely circulated coin of the empire, and also the largest in size, is the brass *sestertius*.

The first Roman coin to feature a portrait depicts the general Flaminius, but for a long while after, coins like the one below continued to avoid portraits.

By 55 BCE, coins still featured scenes instead of portraits. This one, showing a female warrior leading a horse, was minted by the triumvir Publius Licinius Crassus. It was soon to change: in the imperial era most coins show a portrait of the reigning emperor.

### Roman coin equivalents

| Coin name | Metal | Equivalent to *aureus* |
|---|---|---|
| *aureus* | gold | 1 |
| *denarius* | silver | 25 |
| *sestertius* | brass | 100 |
| *dupondius* | brass | 200 |
| *as* | bronze | 400 |
| *semis* | brass | 800 |
| *quadrans* | bronze | 1600 |

## Rampant inflation

During the reign of Nero, who spent money lavishly, prices rose alarmingly, so people could buy less and less with their coins. To compensate, Nero dropped the weight and quality of the *denarius*, a cost-cutting practice that has continued under successive emperors. Often, gold and silver coins are made from cheap copper, with only a thin coating of precious metal.

## Banking

Rome controls a huge trading network. Merchants and businessmen who need money to fund trading expeditions go to a money-lender, or banker. Wealthy equestrians run most of the banks. They are sometimes supported by the wealth of their senatorial patrons, who avoid business itself as being beneath their dignity.

Valuables and money are deposited with a banker. He pays a small rate of interest on the deposit in return for lending the money at a higher rate of interest to a merchant who needs funds. The rate of interest is generally 6–10 percent, although it is much higher in the outlying provinces where the investment risk is greater.

There are money-changers (*argentarii*) and bankers all over the empire. Some are controlled by the government, but others are allowed to operate individually. Using bills of exchange between banks, payments can be made from one side of the empire to the other without the physical exchange of money.

## The state treasuries

At one time, like the Greeks, Romans kept the state treasury (*aerarium*) in a temple. In Rome it was the temple of Saturn, so the treasury is known as the *aerarium Saturni*. It is administered by *quaestors* (officials) under the control of the Senate. The *aerarium* is used for depositing cash and archives of the Roman state, but its function as a state treasury has fallen into decline under the emperors.

The imperial treasury is known as the *fiscus*, which is controlled by the emperor and run by fiscal administrators of the imperial civil service. Over the decades, more public money has been diverted to the *iscus* and away from the *aerarium*. In addition, the emperor owns vast estates all over the empire which are collectively called the *patrimonium principis*. Administered by the emperor's procurators on his behalf, this brings in enormous imperial revenue.

From these two sources, the emperor finances the army and any wars, as well as public building programs, such as new baths, forums, or law courts, and finances the maintenance of the empire's roads, bridges, and aqueducts.

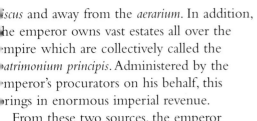

The Roman treasury is located under the Temple of Saturn in the Forum. Using temple basements to store money dates back to the Greeks.

## Making money

In ancient times, the Roman mint was located in the temple of Juno Moneta on the Capitol, from which we derive the word "money." In the imperial period a far larger mint was relocated to premises on the Caelian Hill.

## Monetary equivalents

Equating Roman monetary values with modern ones is not easy, since most modern currencies are no longer related to the gold standard. However, as a rough estimate, the gold aureus is equivalent to about $75. The silver denarius, is worth about $3.

## Weights and measures

Weights and measures are based on natural units, the smallest for measuring the weight of barleycorn. Roman weight is based on the pound or *libra*, which means "balance." Balances are used to weigh bars of bronze *asses* (same as the coins), and so the term *as* is also used for a Roman pound in weight.

Because the bars are a Roman foot in length (11.65 modern inches) and divided into 12 units, the term *as* also means 1 foot, or 12 inches, and so both ounces and inches (*unciae*, from which we derive "ounce") have the same names. Two other terms are familiar from those used for coins. The subdivisions of the pound/foot are:

| | | |
|---|---|---|
| *as* or *libra* | = 1 pound | = 12 *unciae* |
| *deunx* | = 11 ounces | = 11 *unciae* |
| *dextans* | = 10 ounces | = 10 *unciae* |
| *dodrans* | = 9 ounces | = 9 *unciae* |
| *bes* | = 8 ounces | = 8 *unciae* |
| *septunx* | = 7 ounces | = 7 *unciae* |
| *semis* | = 6 ounces | = 6 *unciae* |
| *quincunx* | = 5 ounces | = 5 *unciae* |
| *triens* | = 4 ounces | = 4 *unciae* |
| *quadrans* | = 3 ounces | = 3 *unciae* |
| *sextans* | = 2 ounces | = 2 *unciae* |
| *uncia* (ounce) | = 1 ounce | = 1 *uncia* (inch) |

# The Roman Legal System

In 450 BCE a document called the Twelve Tables was published. From this list of rules and statutes Roman civil law is derived. Romans rely on civil laws to address a variety of issues.

The Twelve Tables cover laws regarding money, property rights, family inheritance, and public behavior. Since its publication Roman law has become far more complex, but the Tables' basic principles remain in force.

## Making new laws

In the Republic, the Senate and various Assemblies made new laws, but their interpretation was down to *praetors*, the magistrates who judged trial cases, as they still do. On taking office, a judge publishes a document called an *edictum perpetuum* listing his interpretation of each law. This fixes how the laws will be interpreted from that point on. In earlier times, his successor in office was not bound by this "perpetual edict." It was only after 67 BCE that a *praetor* was even obliged to honor his own edict, let alone those that came before him.

Now, the emperor devises most new laws, and even those issued by the Senate require his approval. As jurists say, "What pleases the emperor has the force of law."

## The cost of bringing a case

Trials are set in motion by individuals, since the government itself does not prosecute people. However, seeking justice for the individual living in Italy has not always been easy. For centuries, cases could only be tried in Rome, meaning that many people living far away in the north or south had to travel for days to reach the city, and then spend a fortune on food and accommodation for the duration of their stay.

Emperor Hadrian changed this state of affairs. According to his edict, four men of consular rank are givn two or three districts of Italy each to look after. They are circuit judges, known as the *quattuorviri consulares*. This innovation has reduced the often-crippling costs of bringing an appeal to Rome and also relieved pressure on the city's overcrowded courts.

## The flexible law

Roman civil law allows great flexibility in adapting legal principles in the complex society of the empire. Old laws are rarely replaced, but jurists often develop alternative procedures to allow for greater fairness.

For example, a Roman is allowed by law to make his will as he wishes, but if he does not leave his children at least 25 percent of his property a magistrate may let them have the will declared invalid as an "irresponsible testament."

## A day in court

In the provinces, governors act as trial judges, while in Rome praetors manage the courts. These men decide whether or not a case is worthy of trial, then choose a judge or try the case themselves. In Rome, jury trials are held in the great basilicas near the Forum. The jury may vary in number, but in important cases up to 75 citizens will be called to serve.

There is a division between public law (*see page 72*) and private law, which accounts for most trials. Because there is no state prosecution service, it is up to the aggrieved person or family to arrest the perpetrator and bring him to court, as well as any material witnesses. This usually means that the plaintiff and the defendant make their own cases before the judge and jury.

If the matter is serious, the accused may hire an *advocatus* (attorney) to speak on his behalf, usually his patron (*see pages 44–45*). Attorneys do not receive fees but get political help instead. This is why it is important for aspiring politicians to provide assistance to as many people as possible.

If the advocate's rhetorical oratory is unable to persuade the jury, perhaps the accused's family can help. It is common for wives, aunts, grandparents, and children to gather before the jurists in a weeping mass, hoping to make them feel sorry for him. If insufficient family members are available,

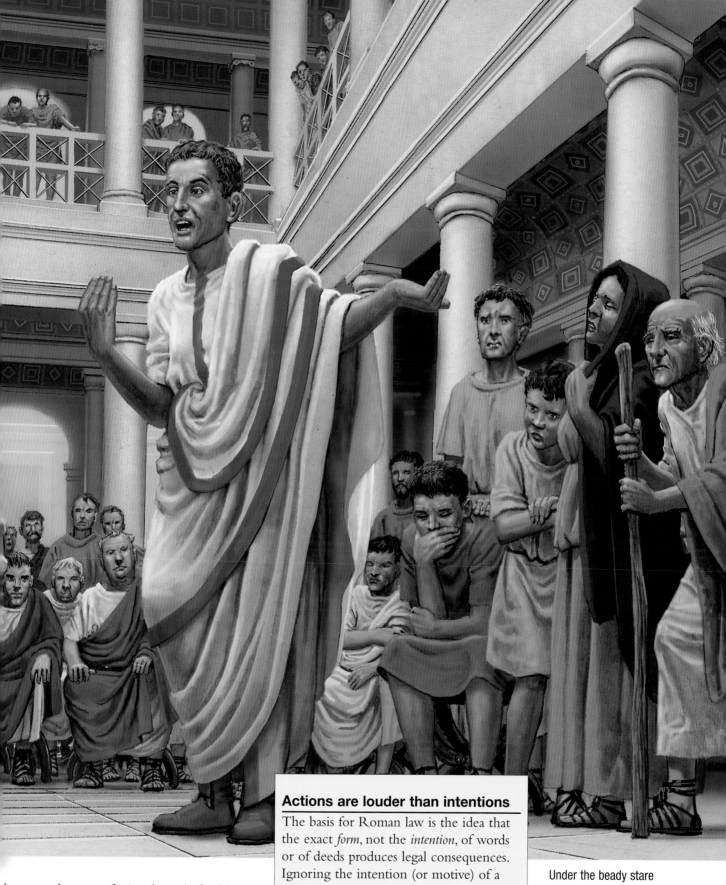

## Actions are louder than intentions

The basis for Roman law is the idea that the exact *form*, not the *intention*, of words or of deeds produces legal consequences. Ignoring the intention (or motive) of a person seems unfair from a modern perspective, but the Romans recognize that there can be witnesses to someone's actions and words, but not to their thinking and intentions.

here are always professionals ready for hire.

Once everyone has had their say, the jury decides by voting whether the accused is guilty or innocent. Then the judge announces the verdict and decides the punishment.

Under the beady stare of the prosecutor, Maximus Valerius pleads for the accused, whose pitifully distraught family adds drama to proceedings.

# Crime and Punishment

Punishment in the Roman legal system distinguishes between public and private crimes, reflecting the division between public and private law. In each case, the punishment is designed to fit the crime.

Punishment depends on the social status of the convicted person. Judges place the accused into one of two categories: *honestiores* and *humiliores*. The first category, the more honest men, includes senators and equestrians, while the *humiliores* are usually poorer, and therefore considered less honest. The severity of the punishment reflects their status.

## Private and public punishment

Civil offenses are dealt with by private law. These crimes include non-payment of debts, not fulfilling contracts, committing fraud, theft, or assault. The punishment is usually the payment of a fine or compensation to the injured party.

Public crimes—effectively crimes against the state—include treason, electoral bribery, embezzlement of state property, adultery, and murder by violence or poison. Separate tribunals are set up to deal with these, and the punishments are severe, with *humiliores* getting the worst of it.

Capital punishment is carried out in a number of ways, depending on the condemned person's status: beheading with a sword (for military personnel), burning alive, crucifixion, exposure to wild animals in the arena, or drowning in a sack.

Punishments also include flogging, *ad metallum* (condemned *to the mines*), banishment to a gladiatorial training school, a life sentence as an oarsman in the navy galleys, and partial or total confiscation of property.

In the case of public punishment, there is no attempt at rehabilitation of the *damnati* (condemned), so Rome has no real prisons. The public prison is reserved as a measure against those disobeying a magistrate's order, and the imprisonment is usually short.

## Exile

When a rich person or a senator is found guilty of a public crime, his punishment might be banishment from Rome. But where *humiliores* will find themselves in the mines or the arena, *honestiores* are treated with greater laxity.

If the wealthy man is condemned to death the magistrate often delays his arrest to give him time to escape into voluntary exile (*exilium*) before his sentence is passed. Nevertheless, he loses his citizenship and his property is confiscated by the state.

In certain cases, the sentence may be *relegatio*, a temporary banishment to a place—often one of the small islands off the Italian coast—without loss of citizenship or estates. *Departatio* is permanent exile to somewhere horrid, with loss of citizenship and confiscation of property. No person within Italy may give aid or shelter to a person who has been exiled

**Right:** Men condemned to death may provide entertainment in the arena by being thrown to wild animals for execution.

**Center right:** A woman convicted of adultery is sewn into a sack and tossed to a watery death in the Tiber.

**Below:** For a wealthy citizen, banishment to a remote place far from the hustle and bustle of beloved Rome is like having their lifeblood cut off.

**Right:** A life sentence as an oarsman in the navy galleys is a difficult fate.

Crucifixion is as cruel a form of execution as any. The victim, tied by his hands or nailed through the palm to a T-shaped cross, dies slowly of asphyxiation—the loss of breath. This punishment is usually reserved for slaves convicted of a crime. The largest mass crucifixion took place in 73 BCE when slaves in Capua revolted under the leadership of the gladiator Spartacus.

## Torture and slaves

Most Romans look after their slaves well but a master may punish his slaves as he sees fit. A harsh owner may have them beaten, mutilated, or branded. If a slave should murder his master or any of his family, all the other slaves in the household are put to death, usually by crucifixion. This is intended to deter possible slave revolts and to encourage slaves to report misdeeds.

During criminal proceedings, any slave ordered to give evidence in court is routinely tortured first. It is believed that the slave would not otherwise tell the court the truth. Although the torture of citizens used to be rare, in the imperial period it has become much more common, in civil cases as well as public.

# The Roman Water Supply

The Romans are not the first to bring water from a distance in aqueducts, but they have turned it into a science. As a consequence Roman citizens have continuous access to clean, fresh water for drinking and washing.

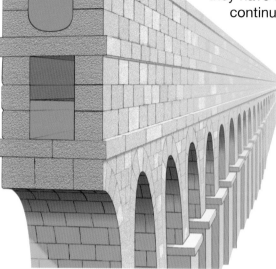

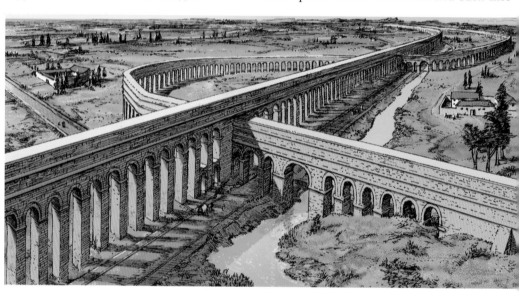

A cross section through the Aqua Claudia, carrying the more modern Aqua Anio Novus above it, as it approaches Rome on an arcade across the plain.

Aqueducts approching Rome meet in a tangle. These two arcades actually carry three water channels each, the most recent at the top. The line of trees at the top marks the route of the Via Appia.

Two aqueducts are fed by the lakes to the north of Rome, and serve the northwestern districts of the city, including the newest, the Aqua Traiana, built by Emperor Trajan, which supplies the region on the west bank of the Tiber.

## How an aqueduct works

An aqueduct relies on gravity, so it is built on a carefully calculated downhill gradient from its source to the city. If necessary, a river valley is crossed by carrying the channel on a bridge. When a long, shallow valley gets in the way, the water is diverted in a series of closed pipes. The pipes pass down one side of the valley and up to a lower point on the other side and back into

Waterproof concrete has made possible the miracle of constant running water for almost all of Rome. Since 312 BCE, when the first aqueduct, the Aqua Appia, was built by the censor Appius Claudius Caecus, no less than nine other major aqueducts have been constructed. Between them, they discharge some 298,000 gallons of water every day.

Only about 10 percent of the aqueducts run above ground, with the rest routed at ground level or below. But it is the graceful arcades that everyone most admires.

The waters of the River Anio from the Apennine foothills to the east of Rome feed all but two of these aqueducts. The Aqua Marcia, completed in 144 BCE, is renowned for the purity of its water. It was the first to be carried across the plain from Tivoli to Rome on an arcade, and cost a great deal of money to build. Money was saved on two later channels, the Aqua Tepulia (125 BCE) and the Aqua Julia (33 BCE), by building them on top of the Aqua Marcia—a triple-decker striding across the plain.

A domestic drain with tiled top (see opposite) at Rome's port of Ostia.

the aqueduct channel. This works on what is known as the "inverted siphon" principle, since water always finds its own level.

The aqueducts require a great deal of maintenance to keep them running. This is the responsibility of the *Cura Aquarum* or Water Department. It employs hundreds of engineers, overseers, and slaves. Inspection chambers are built at regular intervals for checking water levels, purity, and flow. Obstructions can be removed and limescale cleaned from the channel.

**bottom right:** Public
fountains stand at most
intersections. There is
no faucet, and the
water flows into the
basin and then into the
drain. One runs under
every major street,
eventually joining the
*cloaca maxima*—the
great drain. Lead pipes
carry fresh water and
branch pipes supply
fountains, and private
and public buildings.

## Water for bathing and drinking

The principal purpose of the aqueducts is to
supply water to public baths. But thanks to
this continual supply, there are plenty of
public drinking fountains to supply the vast
population that does not enjoy a water
connection at home, and to flush the public
lavatories or *foricae* (*see also page 93*).

An aqueduct arrives in the city at the
highest point, where the water enters a series
of settling tanks to remove any sediment,
before passing into a large distribution
cistern known as a *castellum*. From here, the
water is distributed through the large lead
pipes that supply various parts of the city.

While the water gushing from Rome's
many fountains is free, householders have to
pay for a connection. They are charged
according to the pipe diameter entering their
house, the standard measuring unit being the
*calix*, or nozzle. *Calices* come in several sizes,
depending on how much water the
householder requires.

Taps or valves are rare, and the water
simply runs 24 hours a day, overflowing from
a cistern into the drain. This is usually placed
in the kitchen area of a town house and
probably runs under the nearby latrine
before falling into the civic sewerage system.

## Sophisticated sewers

While a 24-hour water supply is wonderful,
the fact that it never stops running means
that adequate provision for drainage is
essential. Underground sewers, usually built
beneath the streets, carries overflow water
and waste from the latrines.

In Rome the sophisticated system of local
sewers connects to larger channels and
eventually to the *cloaca maxima*, or main
drain. This flows out into the Tiber. Outside
the city, private houses and the larger inns
discharge their overflow water and waste
into a large soakaway called a cesspit.

The sewers are equipped with manholes
at regular intervals that provide access for the
municipal slaves to carry out regular cleaning
and repairs.

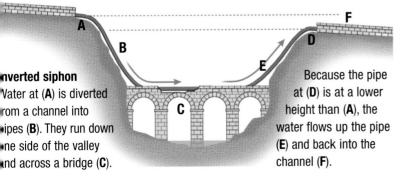

**Inverted siphon**
Water at (**A**) is diverted
from a channel into
pipes (**B**). They run down
one side of the valley
and across a bridge (**C**).

Because the pipe
at (**D**) is at a lower
height than (**A**), the
water flows up the pipe
(**E**) and back into the
channel (**F**).

# CHAPTER 4

# Religion and Relaxation

## Spirits, Deities, and a State Religion

Roman deities fall into two groups. Spirits protect places and are worshipped at home, while gods are worshipped in public and form the state religion.

The state religion grew from the rituals of early farming families who asked the *numina* (natural spirits) to give them healthy children, favorable weather, good harvests, and protect them from enemies. As the farming community expanded priests began to organize these requests on behalf of all the people. In time, the early Romans adopted the more sophisticated Greek gods, built temples to them, and so the state religion emerged.

### Worship at home

Romans believe that their homes are still under the influence of the ancient divine *numina*. Among these ancient spirits the *lares* look after the whole household, the *penates* protect the stores, the family's guardian spirit is called a *genius*, and *manes* are the ancestors.

Some *numina* are shared between all people, such as Vesta, goddess of the hearth, and Janus, god of the doorway, who can look in different directions with his two faces.

### Public worship

Ritual prayers and sacrifice are a part of daily life. The sacrifice—of food offerings or animals—is to please the god, the prayers to ask for good things to happen. Roman priests have no sacred writings other than prayers, so people are free to think and believe what they want about their gods. However, the rituals must be performed correctly. The smallest mistake in a priest's performance ruins the ritual because the displeased god will refuse the sacrifice.

A Roman temple is usually a single room (*cella*) to house the god's cult statue. Ritual ceremonies take place outside on an altar in front of the temple's steps. Temples also contain treasures won in battle or donated by individuals as offerings to the god.

### The priestly colleges

Most priests in Rome are elected from the aristocracy, and it is their honorable duty to serve the state. Priesthoods are arranged in *collegia* (like the commercial trades) of which there are many—only the most distinguished are listed here.

#### Pontifices (pontiffs)

The *collegium pontificorum* controls the state religion under the guidance of the *pontifex maximus* (chief priest). Pontiffs decide the dates of the year's religious days as outlined on page 40 and festivals, preside at formal ceremonies and are also responsible for the *flamines* and the Vestal Virgins.

Each house has a shrine to the *lares* called a *lararium*, where the family prays every day, and offers small gifts of food and drink.

**Opposite:** In this relief from Trajan's Column, a boar and a ram are led toward the altar to be sacrificed. As emperor and *pontifex maximus*, Trajan (extreme top right) presides over the ceremony with his head traditionaly covered. A priest on the left holds the sacrifical hammer ready. In the ritual no mistakes are allowed, or the whole ceremony must be restarted to avoid bad luck. After the sacrifice Augurs will examine the beasts' entrails for signs of godly approval.

Statue of Augustus in the apparel of *pontifex maximus*. His head is covered as sign of religious respect.

## Flamines

A *flamen*, identified by his *apex* (a white conical leather hat) is appointed to serve a particular god. There are 15 *flamines*.

## Augures

These priests interpret signs—known as "auspices"—from the gods, observed in various ways, such as the feeding habits of sacred chickens or the flight patterns of birds. Augurs don't predict the future, they discover if the gods approve a proposed course of action.

## Haruspices

The word *haruspex* means "gut-gazer" and the priests of this college rival the augurs in divining the will of the gods. However, they do so by examining the entrails of sacrificed animals, as well as the effects of lightning, which comes from Jupiter, king of the gods.

## Vestal Virgins

The *pontifex maximus* selects Vestals from girls of high birth aged between six and ten. They serve for 30 years, living in the *Atrium Vestae* (Vestal House) in the Forum. Their duties include tending the sacred fire on the hearth in the temple of Vesta and holding the inheritance wills of citizens. They also guard the Palladium, an image of the Greek goddess Pallas Athena, which protects Rome.

## Salii

The *salii* ("leapers") are the 24 priests of Mars, god of war, whose duty is to dance in procession during his festivals. They dress in archaic military uniforms and carry sacred shields as they dance, singing the ancient hymn called *carmen saliare*.

## Fetiales

A college of priests selected for life from among noble families, the *fetiales* are responsible for the rituals involved in declaring war and making treaties.

## Augustales

This imperial college of priests looks after the worship of the emperor. In the East the people find it natural to worship the living emperor as a god, but in the West he is usually only made a god after his death.

# Gods and Goddesses

There are well over 200 Roman gods and goddesses. Some developed from ancient Roman spirits, others have been absorbed from other cultures and merged with Roman gods.

The major gods, known as the Twelve Great Gods, known as the *Di Consentes*, are the Olympians. They are derived directly from the major gods of the Greeks and have the same relationships to each other. The *Di Consentes* are celebrated in a colonnaded porch which stands at the end of the Forum

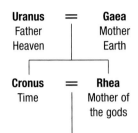

| Uranus | = | Gaea |
|--------|---|------|
| Father |  | Mother |
| Heaven |  | Earth |

| Cronus | = | Rhea |
|--------|---|------|
| Time |  | Mother of the gods |

under the Capitoline Hill. Of these, the three most senior—Jupiter, Juno, and Minerva, known as the Capitoline Triad—also share a temple on the Capitoline Hill. The Roman Olympians are shown in this chart, with their original Greek equivalents in brackets.

**Juno (Hera)**, Jupiter's wife and sister, goddess of childbirth and women. = **Jupiter (Zeus)**, king of the gods, and god of thunder and lightning.

**Neptune (Poseidon)**, god of the sea.

**Dis** or **Pluto (Hades)**, god of the Underworld.

**Vesta (Hestia)**, goddess of the hearth.

**Ceres (Demeter)**, goddess of agriculture (*not one of the Twelve*).

**Vulcan (Hephaestus)**, god of craftsmen and forges.

=

**Venus (Aphrodite)**, goddess of love.

**Mars (Ares)**, god of war.

**Apollo (Apollo)**, god of the sun, music, and prophecy.

**Diana (Artemis)**, goddess of the moon and hunting.

**Minerva (Athena)**, goddess of crafts and war.

**Mercury (Hermes)**, god of trade, thieves, the gods' messenger.

**Bacchus (Dionysus)**, the god of wine, originally formed part of the Roman Olympians, but was later replaced by Vesta.

**Roma**

There are many lesser gods. Several look after fertility and growth, such as Flora and Faunus. Others, such as the god Quirinus and the goddess Bellona, are responsible for war. Cupid, the god of love, has similarities to the Greek Pan, and the goddess Roma is the divine spirit of the city of Rome itself.

## Oriental religions

Traditional Roman cults were concerned with basic issues—relationships between people, with the land, and ancestors. Little attempt was made to explain the mysteries of life and death or offer ways of being good. This is why "mystery cults" from the East have gained ground. They have not replaced the traditional state religion, and most people practice the new teachings while still worshipping the old Roman gods.

Their popularity lies in revealing the secret of life after death for initiates. The mystery cults listed below also require people to take part in ceremonies, in contrast to the state religion where people stand and watch.

## Cybele

The cult of Cybele, also known as the Great Mother (*Magna Mater*) came from Asia Minor in 204 BCE after a prophet warned that without her help Rome would lose the Punic Wars. Mother of all living things, her rites include wild music and dancing, and her priests castrate themselves with flint knives, since only eunuchs may serve her.

## Isis

Isis is the Egyptian mother goddess, whose son Horus avenged the death of his father Osiris. The cult became fashionable in Rome after Julius Caesar brought Cleopatra to the city for a year in 45 BCE. The story of Horus and Osiris is one of death and resurrection, and the cult's mysterious rites have attracted many people.

## Mithras

One of the most popular new cults, Mithraism originated in Persia. It offers life after death and asks initiates to treat other people with respect and kindness. Mithras—sent down to Earth by the Zoroastrian god Ahura Mazda to struggle against evil Ahriman—has to hunt and kill a divine bull, from which all living things spring. It is a secret, men-only cult that holds particular appeal for charioteers and soldiers.

## Judaism

The ancient religion of the Jews holds an appeal for those Romans who desire the depth of a mystery cult. However, its belief in and worship of only one god is considered intolerant by many Romans, and even dangerous, since it refuses worship of the divine emperor. Some view this aspect of the religion as treasonous.

Cybele

Isis

## Christianity

This offspring of Judaism has gained popularity among a large number of Roman citizens, usually of the poorer classes, and also among slaves. Its teaching that earthly life is only a test for a far better life in Heaven after death appeals greatly to the wretched and downtrodden.

Unfortunately, its observance requires the initiates after baptism to worship the one true god and accept no others, so Christianity suffers from the same problems as Judaism. Under Emperor Nero, many Christians were blamed for the Great Fire of Rome in 64 CE and put to death in terrible ways, such as being used as human torches to light his celebratory games.

## Stoicism

Greek stoicism is a philosophy not a mystery cult, but it has been adopted by many in the senatorial class who prefer common-sense to the mysteries of faith religions. This may be a reaction to their loss of political power under the emperors.

Stoicism places man at the center of the universe, and stoics accept that cause has effect, that a person's misfortunes are brought about by themselves or their fellows, not as the result of a capricious god's interference.

A statue of Mithras wrestling with the sacred bull.

# The Major Religious Festivals

With so many gods to honor, Romans celebrate as many as 200 festival days a year. Some are solemn, but most are an excuse for having a good time.

There are three types of Roman *feriae* or festival. *Feriae stativae* are annual festivals which occur on fixed days, *feriae conceptivae* are those with dates that are set yearly by priests or magistrates, and *feriae imperativae* are irregular holidays proclaimed by consuls, praetors, or the emperor to celebrate military victories. This list only gives some of the more important festivals.

## JANUARY

### Kalendis Ianuaris (January 1)
New consuls are sworn in and bulls are sacrificed to Jupiter. The Anno Novo (New Year) is dedicated to two-headed Janus, who looks back at the old year and ahead to the new. People give gifts and make vows (the origin of New Year resolutions). The day is also sacred to Aesculapius, god of healing, whose temple was dedicated on this day.

### Compitalia (early January)
This celebration of the *lares compitales* (gods of the crossroads) takes place on a single day, between the 3rd to 5th, when farmers decorate altars on their boundaries. In Rome the 265 district chiefs place altars at all crossroads. The city festival lasts three days.

### Iuturnae (January 11)
Festival of Iuturna, goddess of fountains and prophetic waters, celebrated at her temple, where the Aqua Virgo enters the suburbs.

## FEBRUARY

### Parentalia (February 13–21)
The *manes* are honored (*see page 76*). People visit cemeteries with offerings for the hungry dead. No marriages may be performed.

### Lupercalia (February 15)
Two teams of noble youths are smeared with the sacrificed goats' blood. Wearing the goats' hides, they run through the streets, whipping spectators with strips of goatskin to promote fertility.

Compitalia in the countryside and in the city of Rome.

The Lupercalia

### Equirria (February 27)
Established by Romulus in the early days of Rome, this is a festival of horse racing dedicated to Mars, god of war and agriculture. It is also held again on March 14.

## MARCH

### Matronalia (March 1, ancient New Year's Day)
In the Matronalia (festival of Juno Lucina) husbands give gifts to their wives. The 1st to 23rd is the festival of Mars. The *salii* (*see page 77*) dance through the streets and again on the 9th and 23rd.

### Anna Perenna (March 15)
Anna Perenna, goddess of the year, is celebrated by men and women with dancing and drinking—as many cups of wine as the number of years they hope to live.

### Agonalia (March 17)
Also celebrated in December, January, and May, the Agonalia in March is a popular day for young boys to put on their adult togas for the first time.

### Tubilustrium (March 19–23)
As the *salii* dance, the sacred trumpets of war (*tubae*) are purified to bring success in the coming battle season.

## APRIL

### Ludi Magalenses (April 4–10)
The *Megalesia*, dedicated to Cybele (*see page 79*), is celebrated by games.

### Ludi Ceriales or Cerealia (April 12–19)
The *Cerealia* celebrates Ceres, goddess of corn, with eight days of games. On the last day foxes are ritually released into the Circus with flaming brands attached to their tails.

### Fordicidia (April 15)
To promote the fertility of cows and fields, 30 pregnant cows are sacrificed. The unborn calves are burned and their ashes are taken by the Vestal Virgins for use in the Parilia.

### Parilia (April 21)
An ancient festival for the purification of sheep and shepherds, it is celebrated all over

Rome as the city's birthday. Large bonfires are lit and offerings of food thrown on them. At the priestly fire, the ashes of the Fordicidia calves are sprinkled on the flames.

### Vinalia Prioria (April 23)

In the first of two wine festivals (the other is on August 19), the first jars of wine from the previous year are offered to Jupiter before men may taste the vintage.

### Ludi Florales (April 27–May 2)

The festival of Flora, goddess of flowers and spring, lasts six days, with carnival and games.

## MAY

### Lemuria (May 9, 11, and 13)

The Lemuria is a three-day ritual held in every house to pacify the *lemures*, spirits of the household dead. As even-numbered days are unlucky, it is held on odd-numbered days.

### Mercurius (May 15)

Festival of Mercury, celebrated by traders.

## JUNE

### Carna (June 1)

Festival of Carna, goddess of door hinges. She wards off *stirges* (vampires) from babies who are left unattended in their cribs.

**Vestalia (June 9)**, the festival of Vesta.

### Matralia (June 11)

The festival of mothers is held in honor of the goddess Mater Matuta.

## JULY

### Ludi Apollinares (July 3–13)

Originally a one-day festival of Apollo, this has become extended and is now an excuse for theatrical shows, games, and races.

### Ludi Victoriae Caesaris (July 20–30)

A festival of games in honor of Julius Caesar.

## AUGUST

### Vinalia Rustica (August 19)

This festival celebrates the start of the grape harvest, in which the first grapes are picked.

### Volcanalia (August 23)

The festival of the god Vulcan.

The Ludi Florales

Masters serve their slaves on the first day of the Saturnalia.

## SEPTEMBER

### Ludi Romani (September 5–19)

Also called the *ludi magni* because of their importance and extent, these games are held in honor of Jupiter Optimus Maximus, the most senior form of Jupiter. On the 13th a cow is sacrificed at Jupiter's temple and the Senate eat a banquet there, in company with dressed statues of Jupiter, Juno, and Minerva.

## OCTOBER

### Meditrinalia (October 11)

A festival to celebrate the new wine vintage.

### Fontinalia (October 13)

In honor of the god of springs, Fons, garlands are thrown into springs and placed on wells.

### Armilistrium (October 19)

The festival of purification of arms is held in honor of Mars. The *salii* dance in procession as the arms are purified and put away at the end of the army campaigning season.

## NOVEMBER

### Ludi Plebeii (November 4–17)

Theater, games, and races mark this feast of the Plebeian Games to Jupiter. On the 13th a banquet is held for senators and magistrates.

## DECEMBER

### Bona Dea (December 3)

This festival in honor of the "Good Goddess" is not held in her temple, but in the house of a consul with only women present. Men are strictly forbidden to see any of the secret rites.

### Agonalia (December 11)

Also the Septimontium, a festival in honor of the seven hills of Rome.

### Saturnalia (December 17–23)

This important festival honors Saturn, god of seed sowing. On the first day, after a sacrifice of pigs at the temple of Saturn, work ceases and the feasting begins.

Gambling in public (otherwise banned) is allowed, and everyone wears holiday clothes. Slaves are given the day off and may even be served by their masters. In time, this festival will be replaced by Christmas.

# In the Arena

The ludi, or Roman games, combine gladiatorial combat with chariot-racing and theatrical shows. The games have religious origins, but for most Romans they are now an excuse for a good day out.

From obscure beginnings as a religious rite, the gladiatorial games (*ludi munera*) are the most dramatic aspect of the Roman taste for entertainment. Men fight for their lives before baying crowds, their blood raked over in the sand before the next combatants enter the amphitheater. The very word *arena* means "sand."

The gladiatorial tradition started among Rome's ancient neighbors, the Etruscans and Samnians, as a funeral rite. The first recorded gladiatorial combat in Rome took place in 264 BCE, when three pairs of gladiators (users of the *gladius*, or short sword) fought to the death in the Forum Boarium at the funeral of Decimus Junius Pera. From this point, the scale and frequency of games increased and now they are exported around the empire. Many provincial towns boast their own amphitheater in which to host games.

## Recruiting gladiators

Gladiators are generally drawn from among the lowborn—criminals, prisoners of war, slaves, and persecuted minorities. A few join the profession by choice, desperate men with no place to go, others enjoy the prestige attached to the games. A gladiator's career is usually brutally short, but the few that survive, such as Publius Ostorius—a veteran of 51 clashes—become national heroes and earn their freedom from the emperor.

Gladiators undergo a lot of training, and there are many state-owned schools, particularly in Campania. The most famous is at Capua, and it was here in 73 BCE that the slave Spartacus led an uprising that grew into a nationwide slave rebellion.

## The combatants

There are four main types of gladiator. The *Thracian* is armed with a curved scimitar and small round shield, the *Samnite* has a short sword, oblong shield, and visored helmet, the *retiarius* is lightly armed with a net and trident or dagger, and the *murmillo* has a fish-crest helmet, oblong shield, and sword.

The fun for the spectators comes from pitting fighters of the different traditions against each other, so that a *murmillo* might fight a *retiarius*.

Games frequently include wild animals in the morning session, usually faced by condemned criminals rather than expensive gladiators.

The Roman world's largest and most famous venue is the Flavian Amphitheater—the Colosseum—started by Emperor Vespasian and completed c.80 CE by his second son, Domitian. A superb example of public building design, it seats 50,000 and permits the grandest of spectacles. One event in Trajan's reign lasted for 117 days and involved 4941 pairs of gladiators.

Murmillo

Thracian

Samnite

Retiarius

# A Day at the Races

For Romans, the greatest spectacle is chariot-racing. It is even more popular than gladiatorial combat and—for the charioteers—no less dangerous. Romans demand spills and thrills, and they get them in the Circus Maximus.

The Circus Maximus is the Roman world's largest racetrack. There has been a racing circuit on the site between the Palatine and Aventine Hills since the city's earliest times, and the races (*ludi circensis*) are the most popular spectator sport of all.

From obscure religious beginnings, racing chariots has become a professional sport.

All the charioteers belong to *factiones* or teams. Once, there were several, but now there are four teams in Rome—the *albata* (whites), *russata* (reds), *veneta* (blues), and *prasina* (greens), named after the colors they wear. Each team has its fans, and unfortunately street brawls between them are common and often very violent.

This reconstruction shows the Circus Maximus in about 300 CE. The imperial palace overlooks the arena on top of the Palatine Hill at the picture's top left.

## ut for a good time

uring the morning the stands begin to fill. nlike the Colosseum and most other enues, in the Circus men and women may t together, and so a day's racing is an pportunity for the entire family to enjoy emselves. The senator Maximus Valerius rives early, so that his son may enjoy the reliminary events—religious tes, mock battles, me wild animal nases—before the ain events of e afternoon's cing.

The Circus Maximus measures almost 2000 by 670 feet, and seats approximately 250,000 spectators.

**1.** Triumphal Arch of Titus. His father Vespasian built it to celebrate his son's victory over the Jews at Jerusalem in 70 CE.

**2.** All that is left of the Circus Maximus today stands here, just stumps of the arches that held up the seating stand.

**3.** The two *metae*, or turning posts. Skilled charioteers always cut in close to the *metae* to take the shortest route around the corners. This is also where most accidents occur. Each *meta* is topped by three tall bronze cones.

**4.** Finishing line with the referee's box above.

**5.** The imperial box for the emperor. It is called the *pulvinator*, from the name given to a cushion, or *pulvinar*, on which divine objects were placed in a temple. Many emperors believe themselves to be gods.

**6.** The long masonry rib that runs down the center of the circus is called the *spina*. It is 1100 feet long and angled to narrow the approach to each turn, making it more dangerous. It is decorated by statues and trophies of war.

**7.** Obelisk of the Egyptian pharaoh Ramesses II dating from the 13th century BCE. It was taken from Egypt by Augustus after he defeated Mark Antony and Queen Cleopatra in 30 CE.

**8.** A raised rack supported seven bronze dolphins and seven large eggs to count the seven race laps. A dolphin is turned head down and an egg raised after the leading chariot completes the turn and crosses the start line.

**9.** The *alba linea* (white line) or start line.

**10.** The first third of the right-hand stand angles inward to give an equal break from the starting gates to the start line.

**11.** The 12 *carceres*, or starting gates. The curved line of arches is not at right-angles to the circus track. This, combined with the angle of the start line and the narrowing of the right-hand stand, gives all 12 charioteers an equal chance to arrive at the start line together, no matter which of the *carceres* they start from.

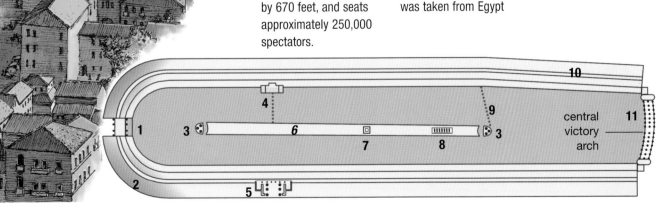

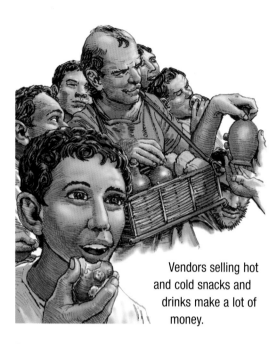

Vendors selling hot and cold snacks and drinks make a lot of money.

## The anticipation grows

The packed spectators buy hot and cold snacks and drinks from numerous roving vendors, who pace up and down the steep rows. Soon, the Circus is full and everyone eager for the afternoon's racing to begin.

The ceremonies begin with a procession (*pompa*) of the charioteers (*aurigae*), team stablehands, musicians, dancers, and priests carrying statues of the gods in whose honor the games are being held. There are 24 races scheduled for the day, and the 12 charioteers draw lots for a position in the starting gates.

This is the moment for last bets. Although gambling in public is forbidden, at the games betting is not only allowed but is a passion, one which Maximus Valerius shares. Men place bets between themselves or with the many agents of the four teams, who run most of the on- and off-track betting. The results of Circus Maximus race meetings are followed around the empire.

Betting becomes furious as the race start nears.

Although most race charioteers are slaves, successful drivers can make their fortunes and buy their own freedom. For most, however, serious injury and even death is common.

The start of a race is signaled when the games' sponsor drops a white cloth (*mappa*). The gates spring open and the 12 teams of horses thunder onto the track.

The strategy is to avoid running too fast at the beginning of the race, since there are seven full laps to be run, but to try to hold a position close to the *spina* and around the *metae* as closely as possible without running—or being pushed—into them.

## Thrills and spills

Races are split into two groups, for two-horse chariots called *bigae*, and four-horse *quadrigae*. The *biga* has a central pole, or "tree," fixed at its lower end to the light

framework on which the rider stands above the rotating axle. The horses' necks are held by a solid yoke, attached by a pivot to the front of the tree. In a *quadriga* the center horses are also yoked to the tree, and the outside horses are attached to the two inner horses by strong traces (straps).

Races are run counter-clockwise. Outside horses run a half-stride ahead of inner horses on the straightaways and are trained to pull outward to keep the team in line. The horse closest to the *spina*—the outside-left—has to be the best trained, especially in *quadriga* races, where it has to drop back a half-stride and pull the others around the corners. However, the outside-right horse should be strongest, since it runs farther and faster around the turns.

The chariots provide little protection for the charioteer, who basically has to balance himself on the axle as he drives. He winds the reins around his chest and waist, and carries a knife to cut through them in case he is thrown from the chariot. This is a frequent occurrence, especially as several teams compete for the inside place at the *metae*.

The noise is deafening, the thunder of flying hooves and wheels competing with the roar of the crowd, each person shouting encouragement and advice at their color and cursing the opposing teams.

Race winners, with a golden palm or wearing the victor's crown, become popular idols and are mobbed by their hysterical fans.

# The Theater and Domestic Games

Roman drama is Greek in origin, and dramatic performances, *ludi scaenici*, were originally staged in honor of a particular god. Over time, like games in the arena or Circus, the theater has become pure entertainment.

Before the late Republic, virtuous Romans thought theaters were a decadent luxury, and permanent theaters were banned. Increasing Greek influence created a greater interest among educated Romans for literature and dramatic performance, and the flimsy wooden structures erected temporarily for a festival became replaced with stone theaters.

Roman theaters are similar to the Greeks', except they are of concrete and stone, far more elaborate and usually much larger. One of the first to be built in Rome, by Pompey the Great, has a seating area (*cavea*) 525 feet in diameter, and it can seat 27,000 people. Some provincial towns, with more space than Rome, boast even larger theaters.

Where the Greeks built into a hillside to create the rise of the *cavea*, Roman architects raise vast substructures to two or three levels. People can enter and exit very quickly through the intricate network of stairs and corridors of the substructure.

## Actors, masks, and plays

As in Greece, the actors wear grotesque masks so their expressions can be easily seen from the back of the theater. The large open mouths of the masks also help to amplify their voices. Most actors are slaves or freedmen—many, in fact, Greek—and the profession is considered to be disreputable. As a result, a professional actor may not hold public office. In contrast to Greece, women are allowed to perform on stage, substituting heavy make-up for a mask.

Comedy and tragedy in the traditional Greek form—once popular—have been overtaken in popularity by mime, pantomime, and bawdy farces. Mime shows are undemanding tales of adventure spiced up with plenty of violence. Pantomime is a little more sophisticated. It typically involves a single *pantomimus* ("one who imitates all things") miming the story's action with the aid of several masks, accompanied by

musicians, a chorus, and dancers.

Romans also enjoy music concerts, which are held in smaller, covered versions of theaters called Odeons. These are also venues for lectures and business conferences.

Each part of the auditorium is reserved for a different class of people. The poorer people sit higher up.

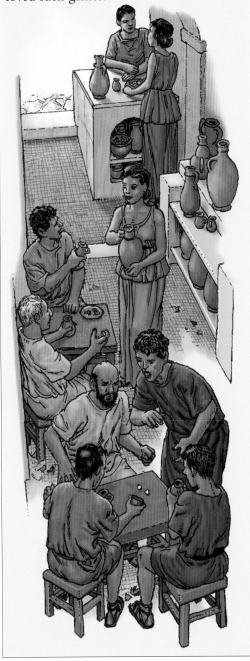

### Thrill of the throw

Gambling in public on the street is forbidden, but Romans are passionate gamblers anyway. Large sums of money are recklessly wagered on a throw of the dice at home, in taverns, or tucked away privately in the baths.

A similar game called *tali* is played with knucklebones made from bone or pottery, and bets are placed by both players and onlookers on the outcome of a board game played with colored counters. Among others, the emperor Augustus loved such games.

The Greek *skene* is called *scaenae frons* in a Roman theater. It is far more elaborate, with two or three stories and up to a hundred columns.

Operators suspend realistic painted scenery backdrops from the upper floor of the *scaenae frons*. These can be changed rapidly for different scenes.

Actors appear on the *pulpitum* (stage). Audience participation is noisy, especially in farces. Booing, hissing, and clapping are continual—fights break out sometimes.

# A Day at the Baths

For the Romans, bathing is a luxury as well as a necessity. The great baths provide a convivial place to socialize, hold business meetings, read a book, take vigorous exercise, relax in beautiful gardens… and get clean.

The first private and public baths were called *balnea*, small suites with individual baths filled and emptied by slaves. The invention of hypocaust heating (*see "Heat under the floor" on page 92*) in the 1st century BCE rapidly led to the development of baths with hot and cold rooms, and bathing became a communal activity.

## Building the baths

Agrippa built the first large public baths in Rome in 25 BCE. The term *thermae* (hot or thermal baths) was coined to describe them. In 33 BCE, there were 170 small baths in Rome; this number has grown to over 850, including the imperial *thermae* of Titus, Trajan, and Caracalla. These are among the most ambitious buildings in the empire.

The water is supplied from purpose-built aqueducts, which also serve local domestic users. The Aqua Traiana supplies the Baths of Trajan, filling a great reservoir known as the Sette Sale. Caracalla's baths, known as the Thermae Antoninianae, draw water from a specially built extension of the Aqua Marcia. The water is stored in a massive cistern to feed the various parts of the complex.

## A series of pools

All the great *thermae* share a similarity of layout. After entering the complex free of charge (privately owned baths charge a small entrance fee, except for children), bathers make their way through the *frigidarium* (cold room) to the *tepidarium* (warm room). Here are found the *apodyteria* (dressing rooms) for men and women. The *tepidarium* does not always have a bath and acts as a general relaxation area and insulates the hot rooms from the cold. It is also a warming preparation for the *caldarium* (hot room). *Caldariae* are capable of achieving temperatures as high as 100°F and are made humid from the hot plunge pools alongside.

Romans do not use soap for washing

## The Baths of Caracalla

**1.** Four entrances, divided between men and women, leading to the main doorways.

**2.** The *apodyterium* (changing room).

**3.** The *frigidarium* (open to the *natatio*, or cold pool).

**4.** The *tepidarium*, or warm room, where patrons enjoy a cleansing session of oiling and scraping of the skin.

**5.** The *caldarium*, or hot room, with 12 steaming hot plunge baths.

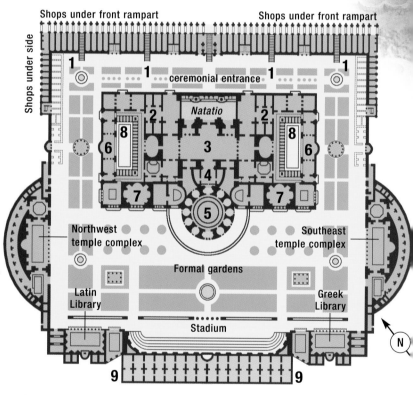

themselves. Instead, bathers rub oil into their skin and then scrape the residue away with a *strigil* (scraper). Wealthy people bring their own slaves to perform this for them, or attendants are on hand to do it for a small fee. The next step is to wash in the hot pool of the *caldarium*. The process is completed by returning to the large *frigidarium* pool for a refreshingly cold plunge.

**6.** Massage rooms.

**7.** Relaxation and private function rooms.

**8.** The *palaestrae* or open-air exercise yards.

**9.** Covered cistern.

Southeast temple complex

Library

Stadium, with seating built against cistern wall

9

Library

**Right:** A flask of scented oil and two *strigils*.

A slave vigorously applies a *strigil* to his master's oiled back.

**Right:** Wealthier patrons take along a slave to guard their clothes against the risk of theft from the *apodyterium*.

## A leisure center

The imperial *thermae* provide space for huge numbers of people—up to 1600 at a time in the Baths of Caracalla—so there are several hot rooms and others for massage. Larger baths have a *laconicum* (hot dry room), a *sudatorium* (hot room to induce sweating), and a *natatio* (outdoor pool). From the *tepidarium*, bathers can walk out into the *palaestra*, a porticoed open-air exercise area similar to those of the Greek *gymnasium*

In addition to the water features and exercise facilities, the imperial *thermae* offer beautifully arranged and tended gardens for walking and contemplation, one or two libraries (Latin and/or Greek), temples and shrines, and sometimes a small sports area. At the Baths of Caracalla, there is even a modestly sized stadium, with seating for spectators built up the sides of the huge water cistern, which is fed by its own aqueduct. With the further addition of conference and meeting rooms for hire, shops, and food stalls, the Roman baths are a complete leisure center complex.

## Heat under the floor

The relaxation and enjoyment available above the bath floors is not echoed alongside and beneath, where a slave force toils to provide warmth for the customers.

Heat to the warm and hot rooms is supplied by a hypocaust system, which introduces hot air (and steam for some rooms) under the suspended floor from a *praefurnium* (furnace) that also heats the water. The floor is supported on numerous *pilae* (small brick pillars) around which the heated air circulates. So efficient is this that the floor needs to be thick to make it bearable to walk on, although wooden sandals are commonly supplied.

The walls are also heated by continuous flues of hollow box-tiles called *tubuli*, fastened to the interior wall behind the plaster or marble facing. The hot air in the underfloor area naturally rises up the tubuli. Holes in the sides of each *tubulus* connect them and allow air to circulate sideways, ensuring even heating.

The *praefurnium* is a fiercely hot, smoky

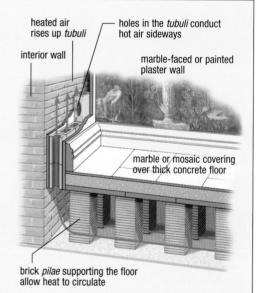

heated air rises up *tubuli*

interior wall

holes in the *tubuli* conduct hot air sideways

marble-faced or painted plaster wall

marble or mosaic covering over thick concrete floor

brick *pilae* supporting the floor allow heat to circulate

environment for the slaves who stoke the fires. They must work in cramped conditions, with small holes in the low passageway ceiling the only means of letting in some light and allowing the thick smoke to escape. The hypocaust is a dreadful place to work for others' enjoyment.

**Left:** Among the younger bathers, the *palaestra* is a popular place for "letting off steam" with a good wrestle before bathing.

**Below left:** Roman sanitary facilities are the envy of the civilized world. In colder regions, a person wishing to sit down will send in a slave ahead to warm up the cold marble seat.

**Right:** Three beautiful wall paintings featuring the ever popular subject of countryside scenes. Note that ruins are already in fashion!

## Amenities for relief

People often spend the entire day in the *thermae*, so *foricae* (public latrines) are basic facilities in all the great baths. Rome is hardly short of them—about 144 *foricae* exist.

They have an open design, with people of both genders seated side by side. Latrines are flushed with waste water from the baths, running in a deep channel under the stone seating. A gutter in front of the seats runs with fresh water for cleaning hands and the communal cleaning sponges.

## A bucolic reminder of the past

More than any other institution, the public baths remind Romans of their origins. The beautiful mosaic floors contain imagery of plants, trees, wild animals, and fish of the rivers and seas. The walls are decorated with paintings depicting rural scenes of agriculture and idyllic hillsides. Even outside, in gardens both formal and artfully natural, Roman citizens can wander among the plants and shrines to ancient spirits of glade and spring and be reminded that they are descended from their honest, hard-working, and virtuous farming communities of old.

# Glossary

**aedile** One of four magistrates in charge of public amenities in Rome, who can be promoted to the office of *praetor*.

**alimenta** A financial service where a farmer or landowner can borrow money based on the value of his land. The interest he is charged on the loan is used to help the poor.

**Assembly** Or General Assembly, where *plebeians* elect officials called **tribunes** who could vote against laws proposed by the *Senate*.

**atrium** A courtyard with a high, open ceiling where people are greeted, the most important room in a *domus*.

**augur** a priest who interprets signs, called **auspices**, from the gods in natural events such as the flight patterns of birds.

**Augustus** The title given to rulers of the Roman Empire. The first emperor, Octavian, was known simply as Augustus when he gained control of Rome in 27 BCE, and it came to mean ruler of the empire.

**aureus** Made of gold, the highest value coin. The silver **denarius** and brass **sestertius** were more commonly used.

**bulla** A good luck charm given to a child to keep evil *numina* at bay.

**castellum** A large water cistern, filled from aqueducts. Pipes take water from the castellum to public and private buildings.

**caupona** A street-side tavern.

**censor** The position above a *consul*, which monitors membership of the *Senate* and *equites*, and holds a census of Roman citizens to determine taxing and voting levels.

**centurion** The senior non-commissioned officer of a century—a company of about 80 legionaries. A centurion is assisted by his **optio**.

**circus** A place where chariot races are held; in the Greek-speaking area the word **hippodrome** is used.

**cognomen** A nickname. Due to the limited number of *praenomina*, people are often referred to by their cognomen.

**cohort** Each legion, or army is divided into ten cohorts, and each cohort consists of six centuries, each led by a *centurion*.

**collegium** A guild or trade association, including the *fabrorum* (builders), *pontificum* (priests), and *pistorum* (bakers), among many.

**consul** One of the two senior magistrates, who in the Roman Republic were elected and served for a year at the head of the government. During the empire, it was an honorary title given by the emperor for as little as two months.

**corvus** A sharp metal "beak" on the end of a bridge lowered from a *quinquereme* into an enemy ship so it can be boarded.

**cursus honorum** The "succession of magistracies," the career path of a Roman politician, beginning as a senator.

**dies comitalis** A type of day when citizens voted in the Assembly. A *praetor* holds a law court on **dies fastus**; both courts and votes are held on **endotercisus**. *Dies atri* is a bad day when neither votes, courts, nor market days (**nundinae**) are held; they are restricted on **dies religiosus**—religious days.

**domus** A city or townhouse, usually of a single floor, owned by a wealthy citizen.

**equites** The middle class of Roman citizens; originally cavalry knights (the name is taken from the Latin for "horse," *equus*).

**fasces** A bundle of rods carried by a *lictor* as a symbol of a magistrate's *imperium*.

**fiscus** The imperial treasury; in Latin a basket or a purse.

**freedman** A slave who has been granted *manumission* by their master.

**gladius** A type of short sword used by a *legionary* or *centurion*, from which the word "gladiator" is derived.

**grammaticus** Secondary or high school, where boys from wealthy families are educated. Grammaticus also refers to a teacher of grammar and language.

**honestiores** Criminals of high status, such as senators, *equites*, and *patricians* who are only punished by banishment, though they may lose their property. Accused members of the lower classes, **humiliores**, may be, flogged, enslaved, or crucified.

**imperium** A magistrate's authority or power.

**insula** A city block. Because multi-story apartment buildings for plebeians usually occupy a whole city block, these are also called *insulae*.

**latifundia** Agricultural estates usually owned by senators and worked by many slaves.

**gatus** A senator or *consul* at the head of a legion; "legate" in English.

**gionary** A member of a legion, army—a soldier.

**ctors** Assistants to magistrates; **paritores** are scribes or junior sistants.

**cterator** A servant or slave who ducates his master's sons and sures they work hard at a *ludus*.

**dus** A primary school. At the age 11, some boys went to *grammaticus*.

**ansiones** Roadside hostels run the state where travellers on ficial business may spend the night.

**nanumission** "Send from the nd"—granting a slave their eedom. However, they usually ntinue to serve their old master in me way.

**omen** A person's family name, or rname; also **gens**, or tribal clan, om which the word "genus" is erived.

**umina** Spirits or ghost that rotect different parts of the lives of omans who honor them.

**ale** A wooden stake. Each *legionary* rries two and uses them as part of defensive fence, or palisade, when army sets up camp.

**alla** A garment draped over a *stola* used as a cloak.

**aterfamilias** "Father of the mily," the man at the head of a ousehold—the Roman version of reece's *kyrios*.

**atrician** A member of Rome's pper class of citizen.

**ilum** A heavy javelin used by a *legionary*, designed to break on impact so enemies cannot throw them back.

**plebeians** Or **plebs**, the lower class of Roman citizen, descended from farmers who gradually gained civil rights and independence from *patricians*.

**pomerium** The sacred boundary of Rome, not necessarily marked by a wall. Anything outside it could be Roman territory but not part of the city.

**praenomen** A person's given or first name.

**praetor** A senior senator with judicial powers, or magistrate, who may become a *consul*.

**Praetorian Guard** Originally the bodyguard of a *praetor*, they defended the emperor and his family.

**quaestor** A senior senator working for the empire in a financial role, who may be promoted to *aedile* or *praetor*.

**quinquereme** A warship with five rows of men on each side; depending on the type, the men handled one or two rows of oars per side.

**rhetoric** The skill of speaking well in public, essential for those wishing to be a lawyer or politician.

**Senate** The ruling body of 600 men, from whom magistrates are elected by the Assembly.

**stola** A floor-length dress made from a single rectangular piece of cloth; the female version of a *toga*.

**synthesis** A comfortable gown worn by the upper class men during dinner and parties.

**taberna** A shop along the outer edge of a *domus* or other city building.

**thermae** Large public bath complexes, divided into frigidarium, tepidarium, and caldarium area for cold, medium, and hot temperatures. Heat is provided by the furnaces of a **hypocaust** underfloor system.

**toga** A garment for men made a single piece of fine white woolen cloth, draped around the body.

**uncia** The basic unit of weight, and also the basic unit of length.

**vigiles** Watchmen of the city who fought fires and also acted as police when they patrolled.

**villa** A countryside home of the wealthy, larger than a *domus*. The residential part is the **villa urbana**, while any agricultural section is the **villa rusticana**.

## Types of Roman roads

Romans have several names to describe roads and streets. These are the most common.

**agger** raised road or causeway over low-lying, marshy ground
**angiportus** narrow street or alley
**clivus** town street on a slope
**crepido** sidewalk
**limes** road or track acting as a frontier boundary
**pervium** throroughfare
**platea** street
**semita** narrow path or lane
**strata** embanked road; after the 3rd century it replaced the word *via*
**via** road or street for vehicles
**vicus** common word for a city street, lane, district, or small town serving a military camp.

# Index